FDR AND THE NEW DEAL

FOR BEGINNERS

FDR AND THE NEW DEAL

FOR BEGINNERS

PAUL BUHLE
Comics by SABRINA JONES
Afterword by HARVEY PEKAR

FOR BEGINNERS®

an imprint of Steerforth Press
Hanover, New Hampshire

For Beginners LLC
155 Main Street, Suite 201
Danbury, CT 06810 USA
www.forbeginnersbooks.com

A For Beginners® Documentary Comic Book
Copyright © 2010

Cataloging-in-Publication information is available from the Library of Congress.

ISBN # 978-1-934389-50-8 Trade

Manufactured in the United States of America

For Beginners® and Beginners Documentary Comic Books® are published
by For Beginners LLC.

First Edition

10 9 8 7 6 5 4 3 2 1

Table of Contents

Introduction VII
   These Unhappy Times VIII
   Introductory Note XI

Chapter 1 1
   Before He Was President 2
   A Lonely Member of the Gentry 11
      THE HUDSON VALLEY BOY
      THE FAMILY, THE LAW AND THE DEMOCRATS
      ANOTHER MR. ROOSEVELT GOES TO WASHINGTON
      LIVING WITH DISABILITY
      SOCIAL HEADACHES IN THE ASPIRIN AGE
      GOVERNOR ROOSEVELT
   The Crash of 1929 24
      WALL STREET CRASH, AMERICAN CRISIS
   Happy Days 29
      FDR THE PRESIDENTIAL CANDIDATE
      VICTORY!
      ...AND HOOVER LEAVES A MESS BEHIND

Chapter 2 37
   Crisis 38
   Meeting the Crisis With a New Deal 41
      A NATION WANTS SELF-CONFIDENCE BACK
      GOOD TIMES? BEER AND BREAD, AT LEAST
   Roosevelt's Tree Army 46
      ROOSEVELT THE LONELY LEADER
      PUBLIC ENERGY # 1: ELEANOR ROOSEVELT
      PROBLEMS AND DIVISIONS
      AMERICANS GET RADICAL
      FARM HOLIDAYS AND GENERAL STRIKES
      THE PRESIDENT AND HIS ENEMIES
      EUROPE IN CRISIS
      THE GHOST OF THE MONROE DOCTRINE
      EUROPEAN DEBTS

Chapter 3 65
   Pressure from the Left 66
   Turning Point 69
      OPPOSITION TO THE NEW DEAL—FROM THE GRASS ROOTS OF AMERICA'S COUNTRY CLUBS
      POPULISM, THE REAL (KING FISH) THING
      LABOR'S GIANT STEP
      THE PECULIARITY OF AMERICAN REFORM
      HENRY WALLACE, THE FARMERS' MAN
      THE POPULAR FRONT AGAINST FASCISM

ANTIWAR MOODS
THE ELEANOR FACTOR, CONTINUED
A NEW DEAL FOR INDIANS
THE NEW PUBLIC CULTURE
MONUMENTS OF THE NEW DEAL
THE FACE OF AMERICAN RACISM: J. EDGAR HOOVER

Chapter 4 89
  WPA 90
  New Deal at the Highwater Mark 93

THE REAL (NEW) DEAL
COURT PACKING
LABOR CONSOLIDATES STRENGTHS
THE "ROOSEVELT RECESSION"

  At the Feet of Lincoln 100

RACE AND THE SOUTH
RELIEF AND THE PUBLIC VISION
HEALTH CARE
NEW DEAL FAILURES
THE APPROACH OF WAR
THE APPROACH OF THE 1940 ELECTION

Chapter 5 115
  Doctor Win the War 116

THE WAR AND THE PRESIDENT
THE WAR AND THE SOVIETS
RACE AND THE WAR
THE NEW DEAL COMPLETED?
THE ARSENAL OF DEMOCRACY
FDR, CHURCHILL, STALIN
YALTA
SHADOWS OF THE COLD WAR
HENRY WALLACE, SOUL OF THE NEW DEAL
HARRY TRUMAN AND THE PARTY BOSSES

  Last Days at Warm Springs 134

LOST HOPES

Afterword 139
  FDR As Seen from 2010 140
  Harvey Pekar on FDR's New Deal 142

Bibliography 144
Acknowledgements 145
About the Author and Illustrator 146
The For Beginners Series 147

Introduction

Introductory Note

The writer and artist of this book were moved to the creative act by the election season of 2008 and the inauguration in February, 2009. The campaigns for Barack Obama's nomination and election amid the worst economic crisis since the Great Depression created a popular, democratic and egalitarian excitement that even now, after a considerable letdown, has hardly faded in memory. During those campaigns and the immediate aftermath, the evocation of the 1930s, the Depression and the activities of Franklin Roosevelt but also of the stirrings of a nation in that time and the antifascist war to follow, were almost constant. Every large domestic issue, but especially Health Reform, has since returned the New Deal legacy to the editorial pages and the air waves.

For ourselves, the historical "lessons" that might be learned have often seemed too narrowly drawn. We have sought to recapture events and moods, knowing that a small book cannot replicate the detail of the hundreds of scholarly volumes on the subjects involved. Still, we believe that the mixture of text and comics offers a novel method of truth-telling and question-asking. We hope our readers of every age will share our interest, our enthusiasm, and our admiration: these were crucial years of national life, 1933-45, and must never be forgotten.

Paul Buhle
Sabrina Jones

Chapter One

before **H**E **WAS** **P**res-**i**dent

FRANKLIN DELANO ROOSEVELT COULD EASILY HAVE FOLLOWED IN HIS FOREFATHERS' FOOTSTEPS AS A GENTLEMAN FARMER IN NEW YORK'S HUDSON RIVER VALLEY.

AS PROUD DESCENDANTS OF EARLY DUTCH SETTLERS, THE ROOSEVELTS LOOKED DOWN ON

THE GILDED AGE BUSINESSMEN WHO WERE SUDDENLY RICHER THAN THEM.

FRANKLIN'S MOTHER SARA DEVOTED HERSELF TO OVER-SEEING HER ONLY CHILD'S EDUCATION, SOCIAL LIFE, MARRIAGE AND CAREER.

HE LOVED BOATS.

I'LL GO TO THE NAVAL ACADEMY!

BUT HIS PARENTS FAVORED HARVARD.

AT HARVARD, HE STUDIED JUST ENOUGH, AND EDITED THE VERY PRESTIGIOUS SCHOOL PAPER.

3

4

5

7

1920 FDR RAN — AND LOST — FOR VICE·PRESIDENT WITH JAMES COX.

HE WAS UNFAZED. IT WAS NOT A DEMOCRATIC YEAR.

I MADE A LOT OF IMPORTANT FRIENDS FOR MY NEXT RACE.

THE ROOSEVELTS WERE ENJOYING PRIVATE LIFE AT THEIR "COTTAGE" ON CAMPOBELLO, AN ISLAND OFF THE CANADIAN COAST.

SWIMMING IN THE ICY BAY OF FUNDY

I MUST HAVE CAUGHT A CHILL. I'M GOING TO BED.

HE KEPT GETTING WORSE.

HERE ARE SOME MORE BLANKETS.

I STILL FEEL COLD. AND NOW MY LEGS ARE NUMB.

HE'S GOT A BAD COLD.

THE LOCAL COUNTRY DOCTOR

IT'S A BLOOD CLOT... MASSAGE.

A SURGEON VACATIONING NEARBY

POLIOMYELITIS! THERE IS NO TREATMENT.

A SPECIALIST

A Lonely Member of the Gentry

THE HUDSON VALLEY BOY

Born January 30, 1882, and raised on an estate in Hyde Park, on the Hudson River in upstate New York, Franklin Delano Roosevelt was a true American aristocrat. That is to say, he came from an "old money" family long secure in their social status. For over two centuries, going back to the original white settlement of the area, a handful of families had owned huge parcels of land, built mansions that would have been envied by European counterparts (except that these were new), and interacted with locals as lesser beings. His parents were not nearly as wealthy as some extended family members because his father had lost heavily during the depression of the 1890s. But they had acres of fields, forests, greenhouses, barns, stables, icehouses, and of course servants, from house maids to farm hands. His mother and father set out for Franklin to be a young gentleman, and the families that he knew closely, Roosevelts and Delanos, were almost identical, old-line Hudson Valley clans of mixed Dutch, English or assorted other heritage.

Religion and philanthropy were watchwords for prominent members of these clans. Franklin would grow up an active Episcopalian, remain religiously involved in many ways and continue to enjoy hymn-singing throughout his life. His grandmother, matriarch of the wealthiest family in Newburgh, New York, served as president of the local Associated Charities. Adopting as its motto, "Not alms, but a friend," she was a woman determined to work toward the abolition of all poverty based on unemployment.

These relations also wielded great political power. A more distant ancestor, a sugar merchant, had helped draft the first constitution of New York State. Others included a legislator in the New York state assembly, horse breeders, ship owners, industrialists, and above all country gentlemen. His fifth cousin, Theodore Roosevelt, was already rising in power as New York police chief, mayoral candidate and dynamic political orator, when Franklin was still a teenager.

Compared to these powerful and dynamic personalities, Franklin, an only child, seems to have been shy. He spent his early years as much with adults, mainly his parents and his wealthy relatives, as with children his own age. He even wore long blond curls until he was five and dressed in what was known as a "Lord Fauntleroy" suit, the dandified outfit of the sons of the English aristocracy. His father, fifty-two years old at Franklin's birth, was old enough to be a grandfather, but when not engaged in business ventures, romped with his beloved son through the family estate, hiking, fishing and riding horses. On a business trip to Wisconsin, his father introduced Franklin to bird lore, part of the fascination with nature that the future president had through life. As he grew, his mother remained highly protective, determined to organize every detail of his young life. He was kept at home with tutors, out of school until age fourteen, then sent to Groton, a new prep academy full of other children of extreme privilege.

Groton was a curious place, founded and run by clergyman Endicott Peabody as a center for teaching morals as well as the usual subjects. Young Franklin had to adjust to the change from his sumptuous room in an estate to a cubicle separated from others by a cloth curtain, a tin basin to wash his face, and a rigid schedule set by authorities outside the family. Years later, he adopted daily rituals like using the same razor blade eight times by shifting the blade around for the sharpest edges, a habit that an assistant described as being similar to Franklin's mother saving string: lifelong Yankee habits that must have been reinforced at Groton as "Waste not, want not."

He had entered Groton two years after the rest of his class and faced a bit of ridicule as "Uncle Frank," marking him as a somewhat solitary figure. In time he adjusted, thanks in part to Peabody as a substitute father figure with the reputation of a "Christian Socialist," that is, someone urging upper class responsibility for the fate of the poor and disadvantaged. In this environment, young Franklin seems to have flourished in ways, taking part in the all-important sports competitions. His grades were not, however, especially good, and he remained somewhat of a loner. In Groton school debates, he took views almost exactly opposite those of cousin Theodore Roosevelt, who urged the American wars to conquer parts of the "backward" nonwhite world. Young Franklin argued against the U.S. invasion and occupation of the Philippines, and against the annexation of Hawaii much favored by sugar merchants. Roosevelt wrote to Peabody, years after graduation from Groton, that he counted it "among the blessings of my life that it was given to me in formative years to have the privilege of your guiding hand." It might be that the Franklin Roosevelt of the Depression years was the best pupil of Endicott Peabody after all.

Franklin entered Harvard in 1899 with a number of his Groton classmates. Although he wanted urgently to prove himself on the football field, at 146 pounds he was too light, and he left the freshman team after two weeks. He drove himself into other kinds of extra-curricular activities, including secretary of the Freshman Glee Club. He worked hard to make a mark at the *Harvard Crimson*, the campus newspaper (his clippings included a special interview with Theodore Roosevelt, visiting the school for a lecture). If he remained an indifferent student, outstanding in no subject, and failed to be invited to the most exclusive social club on the all-male campus, he registered in school for a fourth year (unnecessary with his Groton background) so he could edit the *Crimson*. There, his strongest editorials dealt with the Harvard football team and the behavior of the crowds at the games.

THE FAMILY, THE LAW AND THE DEMOCRATS

ELEANOR at 16

Sabrina Jones

It was family life that changed most dramatically for the young man. His father died at seventy-two, after years of heart trouble, in December, 1900. Afterwards, his mother left the family estate for Boston, where she could live in an apartment close to her son. She soon had an emotional rival, of sorts, in his fifth cousin, Eleanor Roosevelt.

The two had "met" on the nursery floor when Eleanor was two and Franklin was five and she rode on his back. She had weathered an unhappy, insecure childhood, with her mother dead when she was only eight and her brother a few weeks after. Her father, an alcoholic, spent much of his time in sanitariums. Probably it was this difficult life that prepared her eagerness to accept a vision gaining popularity among many young women, that of a mission among the unfortunate. By nineteen, she taught in a settlement house and investigated working conditions of women on behalf of a group that would remain close to her heart, the Consumers League. For Franklin she was sweet, tall, and a niece of president Theodore Roosevelt. They fell in love quickly and married in 1905. He was twenty-two, she three years younger. Franklin's mother moved the couple into a New York house on East 36th St., then into a new house on East 65th St., next door to the twin townhouse that Sara Roosevelt had built for herself. The interference of a mother-in-law added to Eleanor's emotional insecurity with three young children to care for in the first five years of their marriage, and even from its early years, it was not an especially happy partnership.

Nor would Franklin Roosevelt have much succeeded as a lawyer—without being a Roosevelt. He seemed an indifferent student at Columbia Law School, but he joined a prominent Wall Street firm on the strength of family ties, played poker at the University Club and on weekends or summers kept up family connections back home like the Hudson River Ice Yacht Club and the St. James Episcopal Church. Bored and restless, armed with a powerful list of introductions to political officeholders, he was invited to run as a Democrat for the New York State Senate in 1910 from his home district. More than anything, he had the family name.

He won narrowly, in an upstate county that the Democrats had not carried in more than twenty years. The way that he won pointed in the direction of his future. He argued for clean government against the political bosses of both parties. And if he spoke poorly at first, he nevertheless seemed to voters a sincere young man who could talk with anyone face to face. It was a good year for Democrats nationally, and for himself as a particular kind of Democrat.

Why was he a Democrat rather than a progressive Republican, like Theodore Roosevelt, or even a conservative Republican? Outside of the Midwest and West, by this time, most liberals had all but given up on the Republican Party, while the Democrats appeared less tied to the South and to the white prejudice on the "race issue" than they had been since the Civil War. Besides, the New York Democrats were eager to get him. He supported shorter working hours for working women and children (voting for a restriction to a staggeringly long fifty-four hours per week), and more significantly, followed cousin Theodore in advocating the conservation of natural resources against the destructive demands of corporate plunderers.

He moved the young family to a mansion near the state capitol of Albany, and quickly found a battle within the Democratic Party, or it found him. Tammany Hall, with generations of clout alongside its reputation for crookedness, was determined to dominate the state legislature, using the Democratic party as its tool. A minority of Democrats refused to go along. Roosevelt, only twenty-nine, became the leader of this rump group, negotiating quietly but also swiftly gaining a national reputation for fighting "bossism." He won no great victories here, except the admiration of his constituents and of liberal-minded readers around the country. These were quite enough.

In one term, he avidly supported the interests of his farming constituency along with clean government, but he made his mark in moral concerns and assistance to the unfortunate. He opposed prize-fighting, then viewed by many reformers as a horribly violent "sport," and his opposition to legalized racetrack betting won the support of the National Christian League for the Promotion of Purity. He supported woman suffrage on the same basis as his support for purer milk for poor children. But he increasingly came to favor more broadly-aimed bills like workmen's compensation. The national mood was swinging in this direction, even if Democrats in many places, the South especially, defended the rights of mill owners and others to offer whatever conditions and pay the desperately poor populations would agree to take.

Re-elected in 1912, he won by a wider margin, and in his district actually ran ahead of the Democrats' presidential and gubernatorial candidates. With his popularity and emerging instinct for political leadership, he introduced motions in the new legislative session to protect farmers in various ways, but also to protect woodlands against exploitation and devastation. Along with his support for protective labor legislation, Roosevelt was already assembling planks in the future New Deal platform. He was on his way in other respects as well.

The four-cornered race for the presidency in 1912 had two major reformers on the ballot: former locomotive fireman, Eugene V. Debs, running his strongest Socialist campaign, and Teddy Roosevelt, also running a strong campaign on the so-called "Bull Moose" (or Progressive Party) ticket. It was a high point of indignation at corrupt politicians and broad public popularity for social progress. Franklin turned aside from his cousin in order to support Woodrow Wilson, the former president of Princeton University, moderately progressive on many issues although deeply committed to racial segregation. The outcome showed that only a candidate with an established machine could win the White House, but Roosevelt's four million votes and Debs' 900,000 suggested the public was ready for change even with Wilson at the helm. Franklin wanted as high an appointed office as possible, and got it: Assistant Secretary of the Navy.

ANOTHER MR. ROOSEVELT GOES TO WASHINGTON

Even as a college boy, Franklin had urged a larger Navy, and now he was in a position to help create it. Lobbying groups for steelmakers and shippers naturally wanted it as well, but so did labor's Samuel Gompers, chief of the American Federation of Labor. A bigger Navy meant more potential union jobs, the marriage of war and commerce that would repeatedly reshape the national economy in the generations ahead. Roosevelt's skill lay in formulating policies at once effectively coordinating purchases and also bringing jobs back to his home state. His mistake was to jump from this influential position back into the electoral arena, in the only failed political campaign of his life: for U.S. Senator from New York in 1914. He had earlier flirted with the idea of running for New York's governor but failed to get the needed backing. He also considered running for the U.S. Senate as a Progressive rather than a Democrat, or running for both nominations simultaneously. In the end, he chose once more to be a Democrat pure and simple. But sly politician Woodrow Wilson characteristically backed the Tammany candidate, who beat Roosevelt badly in the primary. Roosevelt learned that he could not buck the machine.

Back in Washington, he warned Woodrow Wilson in 1916 that "We've got to get into this war," and joined the propaganda blitz to persuade an uncertain public that the conflict was not a battle between empires for more control of the world, as it obviously seemed to be, but something far more ethical. Did Roosevelt himself believe that the United States had the duty as well as the strength to emerge from the conflict as the most powerful nation, military and commercial, on earth? Was he swept away, perhaps influenced by his always bellicose cousin, Theodore, in the wave of patriotic eagerness for combat? It doesn't seem that he asked himself these questions.

Meanwhile, Progressives like Robert M. La Follette of Wisconsin, unsuccessful rival to Theodore Roosevelt's nomination on the Progressive Party ticket for 1912, joined socialists, pacifists and leaders of the woman suffrage movement in urging that the U.S. stay out of any European conflict. Franklin wanted badly to lead troops into battle once the U.S. had declared war in 1917, but instead was assigned to inspect naval stations. If he grew troubled by the unprecedented raids, government arrests and prosecutions of labor, radical and peace organizers during and shortly after the war—the first of the twentieth century "Red Scares" —he seems to have put such issues aside for his own ambition.

For one moment, the Red Scare almost touched did him. Woodrow Wilson's Attorney General A. Mitchell Palmer directed suppression of antiwar newspapers and organizations, highlighted by the mass arrests of radical labor activists and infiltration of social movements by the new Bureau of Investigation (the future FBI). One branch of anarchists responded by striking out against the powerful. Among a series of bombs delivered to Wall Street financiers, one blew up across the street from the Roosevelts, hurling debris onto their doorstep.

Franklin may have had his own reasons other than career and conscience for not speaking out against the continuing wave of repression. In fall, 1918, returning from Europe, he contracted Spanish influenza and, as his wife unpacked his things, she discovered love letters that he had written to her own social secretary, Lucy Mercer. He barely avoided a divorce (according to a later account by his son Elliott, Franklin's mother had threatened to cut off his access to family assets). Meanwhile, he was nominated in a losing cause, for vice-president behind the mediocre James M. Cox, in the 1920 race. He declared himself a domestic reformer, but he and Cox also sought to win the public to Woodrow Wilson's dream of American involvement and leadership in a League of Nations. Public revulsion at the pointlessness of the war overwhelmed their effort.

LIVING WITH DISABILITY

In summer, 1921, he contracted what was soon diagnosed as poliomyelitis at Compobello, the family's summer home off Canada's New Brunswick coast, and never regained the use of his legs. Later generations of medical historians believe that it was a different, less common disease with similar symptoms, since "polio" most often struck children rather than adults. Whatever the actual illness, the story of the disabled politician is one of the most important in modern American political history.

His mother urged him to abandon politics entirely. That he chose to make it his life can be seen as proof of someone overcoming their disability through determination. He pressed onward, through decades of physical therapy and the use of heavy steel braces or standing with the help of others holding onto him. This physical weakness doubtless further deepened in Roosevelt a sympathy for those betrayed by life's misfortunes but still eager to make themselves good Americans.

His choice of rehabilitation was also crucial, in several ways. Seeking help, he found his answer from a New York friend who recommended a once-popular southern resort village, Warm Springs, Georgia. Known for its supposed curative powers since pre-Columbian days among Indians, the Springs had been developed in the nineteenth century as a train ride from Atlanta, Georgia. The local Meriwether Inn had fallen on hard times when a philanthropist purchased it as a sort of spa for physical rehabilitation, in 1923. Roosevelt first visited in October, 1924, and found that he could use his legs and hip muscles swimming in warm water. Along with sailing, a lifelong passion, the visits to Warm Springs proved nearly his only form of real vacation.

Two years later, he purchased the entire resort with two-thirds of his own share of family money, and made it his own. He visited dozens of times across the rest of his life, often spending holidays there. He enjoyed removing his leg braces, not having to hide his disability in public here, and also enjoyed driving with a specially hand-operated car around the countryside, meeting ordinary rural folk, and likely developing his ideas for the rehabilitation of southern social and economic life in the process.

The "Little White House," a modest building constructed for Roosevelt there in 1932, may have seen the happiest and most relaxed days of his final thirteen years. It was also the site of the long-lasting romantic tryst with his secretary Missy LeHand, a secret (like his paralysis) known well to friends, family and his political world, but unreported by the press in this era of respectful media. Weary of child-bearing and grown emotionally distant, Eleanor accepted the relationship, permitting the lovers to occupy adjoining bedrooms in the White House and to spend special time together in Warm Springs. Roosevelt was not well enough to run for office yet, nor was the country ready for him as leader. Meanwhile, he kept up a steady list of causes, like contributions to the Boy Scouts of America, as a means of maintaining his public presence. He spoke at the 1924 Democratic convention, and made an especially dramatic appearance at the 1928 Democratic convention. By that time, great changes had shaken the country. He would not necessarily have perceived the implications, but a basis for economic-social collapse was in process, as were the social forces needed to support his great accomplishments to come.

SOCIAL HEADACHES IN THE ASPIRIN AGE

Economy Over America

Even while the symptoms remained almost invisible, a monumental financial crisis was steadily growing. The power of banks had centralized the economy into ever fewer corporate hands by the time Roosevelt left Harvard, a process that the government engagement in war, supplying billions of dollars to selected contractors, had accelerated tremendously. The promise of an economic boom fueled by selling goods across the war-torn world hit an early snag. A severe recession opened in the first years of the 1920s, expansion dried up, loans came due, production slowed dramatically, and the smart money turned to Wall Street speculation. Bankers ruled, and even most giant corporations borrowed the money they needed, handing over decision-making to Wall Street financiers. Actual production suffered in many industries, coal mining to garment manufacture. Yet stocks raced upward in ever-wilder speculation.

It seemed nevertheless to millions of Americans of all classes but the poorest classes—the rural poor, nonwhites at large, and workers in various fields struck by crisis—that "happy days" had arrived. The "Aspirin Age" of wild illegal drinking, short skirts, jazz, and a relaxed sexual climate was in full swing. But was all well? Behind the façade of glitter, a handful of corporation specialists in and outside government fretted about looming financial challenges and looked for solutions.

Adolph Dehn

"Oh, dear! Soon it will be winter again and we will have to start worrying about the poor little birds!"

So did groups of ordinary Americans with different ideas about the future of the economy. In the years around 1920, a Nonpartisan League seized political power in North Dakota from the two established parties, selecting favorite candidates from both while using methods and offering programs that look, in retrospect, like New Deal-style mobilizations from below.

Farmers and small town workers met at local events across the state. Anyone could join their new organization for a dollar, and these meetings selected a delegate to endorse a candidate for state office. The platform included state-owned banks, grain elevators and other mechanisms to support farmers, bring down prices, and cut out the unproductive middle man. By

William Gropper

the 1919 legislative session, the NPL controlled both legislative houses and the governorship, and initiated a wide array of programs including workmen's compensation, income and inheritance taxes, home buyers assistance, legal protection for strikers, and the nation's premier mine safety law. By the early 1920s, the movement spread to surrounding states. In Minnesota, the NPL demanded the "conscription of wealth" as a patriotic measure and widescale public ownership of industries. It actually gained a following inside the Republican party until a Farmer-Labor party formed for the 1922 elections. At its head was Senator Henrik Shipstead who, a decade later in the Senate, proposed and campaigned vigorously for an early version of the Social Security Act.

Bits Hayden

The farmer-labor movement failed to make headway toward the dream of a multi-state-based, national third-party movement. But popular former Wisconsin governor and Senator Robert La Follette, leading a Progressive Party ticket for the presidency in 1924, won his home state and ran second in eleven other states, gaining five million votes altogether while running a poor third to Democratic candidate John Davis and Republican victor Calvin "Silent Cal" Coolidge. The Farmer-Labor Party meanwhile held onto Minnesota, and joined by several other state third parties in the middle 1930s, would provide a crucial backbone for programs that Franklin Roosevelt adopted after the "First New Deal" of more moderate reforms had failed. "Fighting Bob" La Follette himself was, despite his 1924 failure and his death in 1926, an important model for a future FDR.

The failure of the Democratic Party in three successive presidential elections from 1920 onward, meanwhile, suggested that the old strengths of that party were fading—in some cases worse than fading. In need of new leadership, the party had also discredited itself in ways that Roosevelt would be hard-put to restore and revamp. One troubling aspect was how Democrats in the South and parts of the Midwest, from the late 1910s onwards, fell prey to or moved willingly into the arms of a reinvigorated Ku Klux Klan. Hatred towards African-Americans had led to lynchings and riots of whites in 1919, and President Woodrow Wilson had made no effort to stop these activities. (Neither did the familiar allies of the Democrats, the leaders of organized labor: AFL president Samuel Gompers blamed "the niggers" for the trouble.)

Democrats, barely united around the demand to repeal Prohibition, the anti-liquor amendment made law in 1919, tried to rally themselves once more for a presidential campaign. Roosevelt embraced Al Smith, governor and leader of New York's Democrats and of his former enemies, the Tammany Hall machine. Roosevelt himself served as floor manager at the 1928 Democratic convention (and Eleanor helped run women's activities). Roosevelt quietly assessed Smith's presidential chances as poor, but allowed himself to be urged by Smith to run for governor of New York State. As Smith himself lost the White House (and even New York State), Roosevelt squeaked through. Building on his own home base upstate while playing ball with the machine in New York did the trick.

"Higher wages, suh, will destroy these people's prosperity!"

Escott

GOVERNOR ROOSEVELT

He inherited a smooth-running administrative operation from Smith, and as an empowered executive, he became widely identified, in popular corporate style, with the initials "FDR" for the first time. But he soon faced a Republican-dominated legislature and found himself in a political stalemate. The crucial question facing his early days remained rural electricity: how to get it, and how to get the electric companies to charge a reasonable rate. In this, he failed, but after Black Friday, 1929, the crash of the stock market, he had bigger problems—and opportunities. As the Depression grew worse, his innovations expanded.

Just two weeks after Herbert Hoover's announcement of the President's Organization on Unemployed Relief, an advisory committee made up exclusively of corporate leaders with no mandate to collect or disburse funds to the needy, Governor Roosevelt called the New York State legislature back into a special ses-

sion with a very different mandate. He asked them to approve his proposal of relief funds "not as a matter of charity, but as a matter of public duty." This set a tone quite unlike that in Washington. The Temporary Emergency Relief Administration (TERA) created funds through investment bonds and matched them to state grants for localities. Work relief was preferred to outright charity. These procedures were later adopted in the New Deal, and so was the administrator, Harry Hopkins, a former social worker who first headed up TERA. In a sense, if only in New

Bits Hayden

York State, the New Deal had already begun.

By 1931, he ushered in limitations of working hours for women and children to six days and a 48-hour week, and brought in Frances Perkins as the labor secretary who would bring honor to his presidency a few years later. Increasingly skilled at working with Republicans as well as Democrats, honest and crooked alike, he won the governorship easily for a second term, carrying 41 of New York State's 48 counties, an unprecedented victory. In office and facing the effects of the Depression across the state, Roosevelt seemed a man in dynamic motion (contrasted, especially, with the staid president Herbert Hoover), not necessarily successful but on the move, seeking to help and encourage. His speeches were widely broadcast in the state and sometimes outside it, the warmth of his sentiment palpable for ordinary working people and farmers. His conservation program, enrolling thousands of unemployed men to refurbish the woodlands devastated by commerce, would prove especially predictive. With the approach of 1932, Roosevelt had made up his mind: this was the time for a presidential run.

Sabrina Jones

HARRY HOPKINS

AS THE DEVASTATION SPREAD, PRESIDENT HOOVER RESPONDED: RELIEF IS THE RESPONSIBILITY OF LOCAL COMMUNITIES AND PRIVATE CHARITIES — NOT THE FEDERAL GOVERNMENT.

GOVERNOR ROOSEVELT PUT NEW YORKERS TO WORK WITH THE TEMPORARY EMERGENCY RELIEF ADMINISTRATION.

IT'S A SOCIAL DUTY, NOT CHARITY.

HOOVER WAS THINKING INSIDE THE BOX OF ECONOMIC ORTHODOXY.

WE MUST BALANCE THE FEDERAL BUDGET

PUBLIC WORKS VETO

POOR RELIEF VETO

EARLY PAYMENT OF VETERANS BONUSES VETO

BUILD ROADS AND PARKS

THIS IS A NATIONAL EMERGENCY! WE NEED A NEW WAY OF THINKING.

UNEMPLOYMENT BENEFITS

OLD-AGE PENSIONS

HYDRO-ELECTRIC POWER

William Gropper

WALL STREET CRASH, AMERICAN CRISIS

Meanwhile, conditions were growing desperate and sections of the American population were definitely on the move. In Chicago, for instance, where flophouses provided a roof over the head of the homeless and a little food that kept them from starvation, the facilities were notoriously dirty, with infectious diseases common. Local Communists led pro-tests by crowds of thousands for improvements, achieving some victories through city government concessions. Meanwhile, anti-eviction campaigns raced through poor neighborhoods of major cities in the East and Midwest, with the cry "Johnny, Go Get a Red!" when a landlord's complaint sent police in for evictions. If crowds gathered, police generally backed away and at least a tenant might gain more time to pay.

The impact was especially vivid in Chicago's increasingly black South Side. Radical ideas might not be popular or even understood, but committees that restored gas, electric and water in apartments won thousands of enthusiastic followers. After an interracial rally on the South Side, Chicago's Mayor Anton Cermak declared a "moratorium" on all overdue rents, and tenants of the South Side hung up signs in their window saying "We do not pay rents" and "Please do not ask us to pay rents." Other cities and towns, especially those with immigrant groups

William Gropper

that had taken part in labor activities of the 1910s and retained "ethnic halls" where political meetings could be held legally, saw similar mobilizations among a variety of mostly immigrant groups.

Contrary to what many radicals thought at the outbreak of the Depression, the private economy was not doomed to final collapse and the working people (or farmers) were not preparing themselves for anything like a revolutionary change of government. Most people appeared stunned by the crisis and desperate just to survive. Outside the cities, hobo "jungles" seemed to spring up everywhere, a few dozen to a thousand people thrown together, surviving in structures made of cardboard boxes or corrugated metal. Many of the residents had been roaming the countryside, hopping freight trains, usually caught and thrown off by railroad "bulls," but often managing to move from place to place, seeking work or at least food and clothing. Thousands of children were among those on the move, especially boys, their parents unable to support them.

But the growth of organized protests and strikes, denounced by the newspapers as the actions of dangerous "reds," increasingly promoted a sense that something could be done. There was deep, well-developed hostility toward corporate wealth—would action follow? Hugely popular films like *The Public Enemy* dramatized the rise of gangsters taking revenge upon an unfair society. The prospect for real, deep-seated change seemed to hang in the air.

AFTER HIS OVERWHELMING REELECTION AS GOVERNOR, FDR BECAME A PRESIDENTIAL CANDIDATE IN JANUARY OF 1932.

ON THE CAMPAIGN TRAIL, HIS SONG WAS

"Happy Days are Here Again"

THAT SPRING, A VERY DIFFERENT GROUP SET OUT ACROSS THE COUNTRY, THAT WOULD ALSO AFFECT THE ELECTION.

SERGEANT WALTER WATERS AT A MEETING OF JOBLESS WWI VETERANS

WE NEED OUR BONUSES NOW. LET'S ALL GO TO WASHINGTON AND MAKE SURE THEY VOTE FOR IT.

ABOUT 300 STARTED OUT FROM PORTLAND, OREGON.

JOIN THE BONUS ARMY

THOUSANDS JOINED IN FROM ACROSS AMERICA.

VETERANS MARCH

ON TO WASHINGTON BONUS ARMY

THE "BONUS ARMY" THAT CAMPED IN DC THAT SUMMER WAS OVER 10,000 STRONG.

IN 1924 WWI VETERANS RECIEVED BONDS FOR ADJUSTED COMPENSATION TO BE PAID IN 1945.

FDR THE PRESIDENTIAL CANDIDATE

Roosevelt's nomination on the Democratic ticket for 1932 was no sure thing. Walter Lippman, the former Socialist who had become the nation's foremost political journalist, his newspaper columns circulated across the country, declared in January that Franklin Roosevelt was ill-suited for the highest office of the land. Roosevelt seemed to him weak, indecisive, lacking in ideas, a kindly fellow who would like to be president but had no true preparation for the responsibilities.

His Democratic rivals were hoping for a deadlocked convention that would block Roosevelt's nomination and thrust attention in another direction. Al Smith, "wet" (anti-Prohibition) candidate of 1928, wanted another try, and FDR's eventual choice for vice-president, Texas senator John Nance Garner, also threw his hat into the ring. Even Newton Baker, Roosevelt's boss in the days when he served as Woodrow Wilson's Secretary of War, seemed to have a shot. But none of these rivals had a popular following.

Roosevelt, undaunted by criticism and rivals, assembled a team whose academic members inspired *New York Times* reporter James Kieran to dub it FDR's "Brains Trust." Columbia professors Raymond Moley, Adolf A. Berle Jr., and Rexford G. Tugwell, among others, were all thinkers with rough blueprints in mind aimed at changing existing socioeconomic arrangements: they believed in social welfare legislation benefiting the poor, if necessary at the expense of the very rich. And although they lacked real power, they could write FDR's speeches. Felix Frankfurter of Harvard Law School, another important source of advice, had written widely about the need for a more regulated economy. The result of this thinking, as far as can be determined from Roosevelt's declarations, was for some kind of experimentation.

Former ally and now rival Al Smith snapped that the crisis was no time for "demagogues." As the Democratic convention neared, Smith increased his grip upon delegates of the Northeast closest to financial interests and ethnic voters. Newspaper mogul William Randolph Hearst, whose political career began as an upstart radical, published sympathetic editorials in his papers about the European turn toward fascism, and he supported anyone but Roosevelt, most probably John Nance Garner. As the balloting continued and victory seemed to elude Roosevelt, Garner was offered the vice-presidency, and the Texas and

California delegations put the New York aristocrat over the top. FDR had won, if only barely. Using the radio, broadcasting his ideas in the medium that he would master, he promised Americans a "new deal" if elected. The phrase for an era of American history had been coined.

The campaign proved to be hard-fought, and as much about personalities as about principles. The South was solidly Democratic by tradition, and the West had so few electoral votes that Roosevelt traveled only once to these regions, spending his effort on the East Coast and Midwest. In his speeches and proposals, he echoed the Democratic platform faithfully even when it contradicted itself, accusing the Hoover Administration of spending too much, while he also promised relief for the unemployed, more public works and the restoration of agriculture. Still, pledging new programs and laws regulating big business, especially the financial market, was a departure that sounded to many more like Socialist candidate Norman Thomas than like Democrats of the past.

Actually, Roosevelt was closer to the "progressive" Republicans of the 1910s-20s who failed to capture the favorite party of business but remained especially influential in the West. Senator George Norris of Nebraska, champion of publicly owned utilities (especially sources of water for farm use), crossed party lines to endorse Roosevelt, and through Norris, Roosevelt reached out to Republican liberals at large in many parts of the country. He also reached famously for the would-be voters of Norman Thomas, the charismatic minister who, many thought, would win millions of voters in 1932. Their hearts may have been with Thomas but the majority of their votes went to Roosevelt.

The desultory state of Herbert Hoover's campaign told a very different story. The more he attacked his opponents, the more popular he made Roosevelt, and when he told a Detroit audience that the economy was recovering swiftly, they booed him. On election day, Republicans were treated to the kind of drubbing they would not get again many times in the twentieth century or beyond. 42 states went for FDR and his party won both Senate and House. Now it would be their fault, in the eyes of many, if the nation failed to recover.

VICTORY!

The election itself was, in many ways, one of those turning points in American political history, a moment that seemed to increase in importance looking back in later years, not least a full 76 years later, during the election of 2008. For many observers during the late 1930s, however, the 1936 campaign contained more momentousness, greater contrasts between Democrats and Republicans, and a far greater identification of voters with Franklin Roosevelt himself than the first time around. Still, there were potent signs in the first campaign.

One of the most interesting was the growing importance of that newest American media phenomenon, the movies. During the 1920s, Los Angeles had suddenly become the film-making capital of the world, adding sound films at the close of the decade. The white and Protestant population of Southern California was politically ambivalent, swinging from one party to the other, but for the most part, deeply conservative on issues like race and labor unionism (California's racial minorities were excluded from the political process). The new movie colony was guided by Jewish immigrants coming west to work in favorable year-round filming conditions, with cheap land, low wages and few other restraints upon their productions. As the election approached, a handful of the shrewdest film moguls shifted deftly into the Roosevelt camp and brought their know-how along. Jack Warner of Warner Brothers, later famous for "social" films, used his influence and money to stage a "Motion Picture Electrical Parade and Sports Pageant" at the Los Angeles Olympic Stadium in September, 1932. Movie stars and crowds turned out to support Roosevelt. Filmmakers, still making fair profits in difficult times, were to benefit enormously in many ways from the New Deal, and the wisest of them knew how to make the best of their situation in prestige as well as finances.

Others had more radical aims or hopes, believing the Depression offered proof that the private-enterprise system was doomed. Socialist Norman Thomas, the charismatic former Presbyterian minister, gained nearly 900,000 votes in 1932 and emerged as "Mr. Socialism," a widely respected public figure throughout the Depression. Local election stirrings were at least as important. Floyd Olson, the Farmer-Labor candidate for governor of Minnesota that year, won a stunning victory and declared himself in favor of a cooperative society rather than a revival of corporate capitalism. Dozens of mostly small, industrial towns in German-heavy Pennsylvania and Wisconsin brought socialist candidates into office. Sentiment for a different alternative, labor's own party, swept through egalitarian-minded sections of the badly weakened American Federation of Labor.

...AND HOOVER LEAVES A MESS BEHIND

Meanwhile, with the election past, the last months of Herbert Hoover's presidency proved uninspiring to say the least. The customary "lame duck" December session of Congress found everyone and everything in power discredited. Unemployment in the first month of 1933 was worse, by three million, than the year before. (European conditions were, if anything, even worse.) The sagging U.S. economy dragged the global economy down with it. Hoover emphasized the "war debt" issue, in hopes that reducing and "rescheduling" the money still owed to the U.S. from the First World War would somehow stabilize world currencies (and firm up the collapsed gold standard). This was a phantom expectation. By the end of 1932, bank failure was epidemic across both Europe and the U.S., poorly regulated banks having massively overextended themselves during the

"Sorry to have to be overthrowing the government by force and violence, sir, but—I'd like a raise."

Sabrina Jones

1920s. Small investors lost everything they had, while some financiers successfully turned their money into gold and sent it to European banks. Henry Ford, to take one remarkable example of the self-made American businessman, demanded the return of $25 million from the Bank of Detroit. (Michigan's governor responded by declaring a "bank holiday," closing all the institutions in the state.) Money and credit disappeared from the economy.

Hoover now declared he would make no bold moves without Roosevelt's agreement, while continuing to believe that the election of a Democratic Congress in 1930 stalled a recovery based on a collective self-confidence in the global business community. The most lasting memory, for many, was the Bonus Army that had marched across the country from various directions, bringing veterans of the First World War to plead with Congress for immediate payment of the $1000 bond not set to mature until 1945. While some fifteen thousand Bonus Marchers remained encamped, Hoover refused to meet with their representatives and local officials made plans to force their departure.

Over the objections of the District of Columbia's chief of police, four cavalry regiments, an equal number of infantry companies, six tanks and a motorized machine gun squad moved against the marchers on July 28. General Douglas MacArthur commanded them from horseback and General George Patton directed the tanks. The unarmed veterans, many still in their First World War uniforms and flying American flags, were brutally attacked, two of them (and a child) killed, as veterans and bystanders were showered with tear gas and wounded by bayonets and military gunfire. At least a thousand were injured. In the last days of his 1932 campaign, speaking in St. Paul, Minnesota, President Hoover congratulated himself: "Thank God, we still have a government that knows how to deal with a mob." Neither he nor Douglas MacArthur ever apologized for the savage and pointless action. It was dramatic proof of an ugliness at large, an ugliness for which the new president, himself the personification of the older American gentry disappearing from national leadership, would have to find a cure.

Chapter 2

Crisis

BY FEBRUARY 1933, ONE QUARTER OF THE NATION'S BANKS HAD COLLAPSED AS PEOPLE RUSHED TO WITHDRAW.

IT FELT SAFER TO HOLD ON TO YOUR CASH OR GOLD.

32 STATES DECLARED "BANK HOLIDAYS", CLOSING BANKS IN AN ATTEMPT TO HALT THE PANIC.

ROOSEVELT KEPT HIS DISTANCE.

HOOVER IMPLORED THE PRESIDENT-ELECT TO

MAKE A JOINT STATEMENT ON THE CRISIS.

UNTIL NOON ON MARCH FOURTH, THIS BABY IS *HOOVER'S.*

NEVER BEFORE HAD A PRESIDENT ADDRESSED AMERICANS WITH SUCH WINNING FAMILIARITY.

THE PRESS DUBBED IT A "FIRESIDE CHAT."

THE NEXT MORNING, PEOPLE LINED UP TO PUT THEIR MONEY BACK IN THE BANKS.

THE PANIC WAS OVER.

LETTERS POURED INTO THE WHITE HOUSE AT TEN TIMES THE RATE THEY HAD FOR HOOVER.

U.S. MAIL

BUT STABILIZING BANKS AND INSPIRING CONFIDENCE WERE NOT ENOUGH TO FIX THE FLOUNDERING ECONOMY.

Meeting the Crisis With a New Deal

A NATION WANTS SELF-CONFIDENCE BACK

The socioeconomic circumstances that met the new U.S. president were, for many Americans, almost beyond belief, and governance no more believable. Conditions had grown more desperate since the summer of 1932 and still worse since the elections, in no small part because most of those in office had insisted that maintaining fiscal discipline outweighed alleviating poverty so severe starvation in some quarters was a looming threat.

The psychological impact of the Depression meanwhile deepened. In the wealthy classes in particular but extending far into the population below, the sense grew that traditional marketplace freedoms might not be the foundation of individual liberty. For a society used to resolving its problems through expansion —territorial or economic —this was a lasting shock with a large potential for counter-shock. Changes needed to be made. But into generations of the future, conservatives and conservative-minded liberals would argue that true "reform" would roll back government protections and benefits for the less fortunate. And not even many of the ardent reformers of the 1930s were certain that racial minorities should or could be offered similar protections.

Nowhere was this more true than in the South, where the landowners and businessmen who dominated state and local government also believed religiously in holding down taxes on themselves. They continued to deny voting rights to African-Americans and to poor whites who might upset their rule. Starvation stalked the Cotton Belt and across the upper South, and the American Friends Service Committee reported that it had ceased to be able to provide food to everyone except those more than ten percent under weights normal for their height. Meanwhile, the "Dust Bowl," created by a combination of land misuse and dry summers, expanded dramatically in scope. Here, not even crops for family survival could be grown. Mexican-Americans —those who escaped being deported in large numbers from the Southwest and residing in a few northern cities like Chicago —were in much the same sad situation as African-Americans, often treated as worthless people to be deprived, cheated and if possible moved somewhere else by local officials.

Herbert Hoover's Reconstruction Finance Corporation (RFC), created in 1932 to provide three hundred million dollars to states for welfare, also demanded that the states prove their ability to disburse funds—or lose the money. Even as the new president settled into his office in February, 1933, both Republican and Democratic bankers told a Senate Finance committee that government spending must be *cut* if the system were to survive.

A great public unease having set in, crowds at the inauguration of Franklin Roosevelt on March 4, 1933, were strangely quiet. Only once did they burst out in applause, when in closing his address, the new president promised the use of executive power "as great as the power that would be given to me if we were in fact invaded by a foreign foe." Eleanor Roosevelt recalled, of the mood a few hours later, a sense that people would "do anything—if only someone told them what to do." Parts of Europe were moving toward dictatorships and columnist Walter Lippman urged Roosevelt to take complete power. Indeed, a Senate resolution proposed offering him "ultimate power." Americans wondered if democracy in the traditional and constitutional sense might be coming to an end.

An assassination attempt had been made upon Roosevelt's life only weeks earlier, as he traveled in an open car through the streets of Miami, Florida. Chicago's mayor Anton Cermak, riding with him, was hit (he died of his wounds three weeks later), but the president-elect declined to leave the scene, riding with the mayor to the hospital and offering encouragement. Roosevelt returned to Manhattan afterward, where a thousand armed policemen surrounded him, but the President had demonstrated his personal courage. Disorder continued to spread, but he refused to show the least sign of panic. Instead, he quietly built confidence among a diverse group of potential advisors, differing amongst each other along party and regional lines. Only the poor themselves, and of course minorities, were absent, while Frances Perkins was named Labor Secretary, the first woman to ever appointed to the Cabinet.

Roosevelt's next public expressions seemed to shift toward the public mood. In his first Fireside Chat, broadcast on the radio (but also heard live on the east side of the Capitol building), he said that the "unscrupulous money changers" and the "rulers of the exchange of mankind's goods" had actually brought on the Depression. It may have been the most radical statement uttered in the White House since Abraham Lincoln had declared that Southern slaves were free.

Today's Americans, he told them, had to rebuild a nation where social values would count for more than profit, where the "joy of achievement and thrill of creative effort" would hold more worth than the "mere possession of money." His tone was populistic and strong, evoking almost half a million letters, the overwhelmingly majority of them positive.

His next moves confounded conservatives and liberals alike, adding up to a "First Hundred Days" that formed one of the most dramatic episodes in all American political history, not so much in what was accomplished as in what was proposed. The new president had few bold ideas of his own, but he was eager to learn, and he moved quickly to meet the multiple crises. That his solutions did not carry the country far forward until another series of crises all but compelled him to do so is another matter.

GOOD TIMES? BEER AND BREAD, AT LEAST

The earliest of Roosevelt's moves most likely to be ignored by anyone who did not live through the era was also among the most memorable to those on hand: the repeal of Prohibition. Enacted in 1919 through an extended constitutional process of support from state legislatures, the Nineteenth Amendment had been considered a victory of "purity" over "sin." It was also one of the last major victories of a diminishing, nativist rural population, uneasy about

Frank Davidson

the presence of immigrants from Southern, Eastern and Central Europe (Germans in particular) who considered alcohol consumption a normal part of social and family life. Prohibition had produced in practice an upswelling of organized crime through the sales of liquor, and also prompted the widespread use of amateur-made or mob-made drinks seriously dangerous to public health. Democrats had promised since the later 1920s to bring repeal, and while he could not personally end the constitutional ban, Roosevelt announced on March 12, 1933, his wish for Congress to restore the legality of 3.2% alcoholic drinks (that is to say, a mild beer). Members of the House of Representatives chanted "Vote-Vote-We Want Beer" when the bill was read the next day. It was overwhelmingly popular, a boost to his already great popularity; it promised "good times," rising tax revenues for state and local governments, and perhaps a lessened impact of organized crime upon a troubled nation. FDR jested with the press that if he could only bring through reforms of beer, the economy and the banks, he would have accomplished much—unless they didn't consider repeal to be a constructive act. One down and two to go.

One week before the beer announcement, on March 5, the President called for Congress to meet in an emergency session to deal with the crisis in the banking system; a four-day "bank holiday" was declared on the following day. Roosevelt went on the radio to offer depositors confidence in the safety of their savings accounts. The Reconstruction Finance Corporation purchased shares of preferred stock in banks considered solvent, and thousands of these banks reopened in the following weeks. A public, now greatly calmed, no longer demanded to withdraw its money. Meanwhile, the Emergency Banking Act, guaranteeing bank deposits up to $2500 through a new Federal Deposit Insurance Corporation, passed Congress and rapidly became another of the most popular measures of the New Deal. The accompanying Glass-Steagall Act more closely regulated bank operations (the decisive provisions of this act would be repealed during the 1990s by another Democratic administration). The Revenue Act, establishing the principle of progressive taxation, was passed in 1935.

Roosevelt also acted swiftly with a favorite measure from his gubernatorial years in New York: massive reforestation. The first widescale "make-work" jobs program to engage and pay the unemployed, it created a different kind of army in the tradition of that legendary nonviolent American hero, Johnny Appleseed (born John Chapman) who had planted apple seeds along the nineteenth-century frontier. The creation of the Civilian Conservation Corps (CCC), as requested of Congress on March 31, would enroll a quarter million young men in soil conservation, flood control and reforestation on public lands. And it had two entwined, almost irresistible goals: first to conserve natural resources, and second, to place the unemployed into healthy surroundings, with some small pay. Workers on the CCC made only $30 per month, $22 to $25 of which had to be sent to their families, but for the desperate, this was a godsend. At its highest point in 1935, the CCC actually employed a half-million people, with an average age of eighteen, in 2,500 camps around the country.

The CCC proved to be one of the New Deal's most appreciated programs and one that Roosevelt regarded as based on his own vision. But it faced major disciplinary problems and what was worse, most camps were completely segregated, especially at the outset. Where it existed, African-American participation was limited, especially in the South where large landowners resisted anything that might draw cheap labor away from their plantations. Gradually, segregation within the camps eased, although mostly outside the South. In the process, the CCC "boys" had created thousands of trails and camp-grounds, fire breaks and other improvements, opening the national parks to millions of visitors. This work remained a symbol of what might be accomplished if the usual exploitative objectives of corporations for land use, mining or as dumping grounds for industrial operations, could be restrained for the public good. Small businesses and communities close by the parks benefited greatly as the popular "tourist destination" was born.

There was one more, largely symbolic early victory of the CCC. The brutal crushing of the Bonus Army had blackened the name of the Hoover Administration, and Eleanor Roosevelt personally marked the White House changeover by welcoming representatives of a veterans' contingent to meet and talk. The membership requirements of the CCC were broadened in terms of age limits (and also in terms of marriage). The vets readily adopted the "corps" life as a continuation of their long-past Army duties, and if they only got $30/month like the young men around them, they got good, nutritious meals and healthy outdoor exercise, adjusted downward for those no longer hardy. Like other CCC members, they put on muscle and healthy pounds, found time for leisure and even reading after work, and generally enjoyed what they had been offered by the new, kindly administration.

ONE OF THE FIRST AND BEST LOVED
NEW DEAL PROGRAMS WAS THE
CIVILIAN CONSERVATION CORPS
(CCC) ALSO KNOWN AS

ROOSEVELT'S TREE ARMY

WITHIN A MONTH, THOUSANDS OF YOUNG MEN WENT FROM RELIEF LINES TO ARMY RUN CAMPS IN NATIONAL FORESTS TO PLANT TREES AND FIGHT SOIL EROSION.

WE ARE CONSERVING NOT ONLY OUR NATURAL RESOURCES BUT OUR HUMAN RESOURCES.

IT WAS HIS PET PROJECT.

I'M A TREE FARMER FROM THE HUDSON VALLEY!

ENROLLEES RECEIVED $30 A MONTH, $25 OF WHICH WAS SENT DIRECTLY HOME TO THEIR FAMILIES.

AT FIRST, LABOR UNIONS OBJECTED TO THE LOW PAY AND REGIMENTATION. FDR WON THEM OVER BY APPOINTING A LABOR LEADER AS DIRECTOR. ROBERT FECHNER OF THE AMERICAN FEDERATION OF LABOR

46

WE STILL ENJOY THE FRUITS OF THEIR LABOR IN OUR NATIONAL, STATE AND COUNTY PARKS AND FORESTS.

IN NINE YEARS, THEY PLANTED OVER THREE BILLION TREES.

THEIR WORK PREVENTED SOIL EROSION AND CONTROLED FLOODING.

THEY FOUGHT FIRES, BUILT FIRE TOWERS AND FIRE ROADS.

THEY STRUNG MILES OF TELEPHONE CABLES.

THEY BUILT CAMPGROUNDS AND HIKING TRAILS.

THEY RESPONDED TO DISASTERS: HURRICANES, FLOODS AND FIRES.

MANY ENROLLEES WERE MALNOURISHED. THEY GAINED ON AVERAGE TWELVE POUNDS.

MANY HAD NEVER FINISHED HIGH SCHOOL OR EVEN LEARNED TO READ. THEY TOOK FREE CLASSES AFTER WORK.

AFRICAN AMERICANS RECEIVED EQUAL PAY, BUT THEY LIVED AND WORKED IN SEGREGATED CAMPS.

WOMEN WERE NOT INCLUDED. ELEANOR ROOSEVELT'S EFFORTS AT PARITY WERE RIDICULED AS

SHE-SHE-SHE CAMPS!

UNEMPLOYED WOMEN

IN 1935 (AN ELECTION YEAR) FDR TRIED TO CUT BACK, TO BALANCE THE BUDGET. CONGRESS OBJECTED VEHEMENTLY. THERE WERE MATERIAL AND HUMAN BENEFITS IN EVERY STATE.

OK - WE'LL KEEP IT!

THE CCC LASTED UNTIL THE OUTBREAK OF WWII. BY THEN, OVER 2.5 MILLION MEN HAD SERVED IN OVER 4,500 CAMPS.

ROOSEVELT THE LONELY LEADER

All this came at enormous personal cost. Roosevelt's strength of character might be measured in his private struggle with his damaged physical frame. He told an intimate friend, years later, that the effort to move a single toe for a time during the 1920s had prompted his aggressive strides in his early presidency, still in pain but with his face pointed always forward. He exuded a personal magnetism, and those experts around him felt themselves moved to work endless hours, from the external fight with Republicans over the budget to the internal confusion to sort out the work of potentially overlapping agencies. Raymond Moley, an intimate advisor and friend, called him "the fairy tale prince who didn't know how to shudder" even when facing the longest odds. Eleanor, wandering in and out of his office to point out certain passages of bills or regulations for him to examine more closely, often seemed to give that inner strength a direction and keenness otherwise lacking. They were a team in motion.

Measured in other terms, the Civil Works Administration (CWA) established in early November, 1933, under the mandate of the National Industrial Recovery Act (NIRA) passed in June, was a remarkable success. It created more work, at one stroke, than any other government program in American history —something like 4.3 million at its peak in early 1934. Under Harry Hopkins' direction, two million of these people were exempted from the "means test" by which applicants would need to be on government relief already in order to be eligible for work. And all were to be paid in PWA wage scales, a minimum of 40 cents per hour, tiny by today's standard but a difference of life and death then, and for some, even a little fun. When a movie cost a dime, millions of Americans doing government work could enjoy themselves at night or on weekends without taking away food from their tables.

The CWA set out to build roads, schools and other public works. But such unique programs as the College Student Aid were added, a measure that made higher education possible for tens of thousands of aspiring students.

The CWA's net effect was to hearten a large class of men and many women (since women were not defined as heads of households, they were mostly excluded early on) with the sense that they were doing something, not merely getting government relief. Challenged by conservatives who complained that WPA workers earned too much money, Harry Hopkins answered that "people who want to lower the scale and bring it down are people who have maintained their existence through the payment of low wages" to employees, and that the New Deal programs meant "a larger distribution of this world's goods in the hands of the workers" rather than in the hands of the already comfortable upper classes.

The NIRA, most controversial, also established limits on hours to be worked and protected labor's right to organize legally. Conservatives considered limits on private property rights unconstitutional, and watered down the bill, yet its passage had monumental importance by showing the intent of lawmakers.

PUBLIC ENERGY # 1: ELEANOR ROOSEVELT

In many ways, Eleanor Roosevelt became the great public spirit of this unprecedented effort at social relief. She toured CCC camps, usually without Franklin, and she began speaking on the radio, with six-minute weekly broadcasts. She was paid $3000 weekly for this work and for her column in the *Woman's Home Companion*, money transferred to the American Friends Service Committee, the peace-loving Quaker charity. She traveled far and wide, investigating conditions and speaking to audiences, sometimes in public, more often in private. The press quipped that she was "Public Energy #1," a play upon "Public Enemy #1," a designation offered by the FBI and circulated to apprise citizens of a most-wanted bank robber or other criminal at large.

Eleanor was also very much part of a White House domestic setting that found the President surrounded by staff and family members, not always comfortably. His eldest son James and daughter-in-law Betsy moved into the White House with their small child shortly after inauguration and stayed for years. James often held up his father on stage, but also provided a convenient butt for fatherly humor; Franklin might introduce "My little boy, Jimmy," who was two inches taller, then add that he had more hair than his son, a sort of claim to his own virility in middle age. Among others close at hand, none was closer than Missy LeHand, who continued to accompany him almost everywhere in his travels, work in an office next to him, and sign documents for him.

Missy LeHand rarely spoke to the press, never took credit for ideas, and never suggested to anyone the true intimacy of their relationship.

Roosevelt probably did not expect to spend the rest of his life in the White House. No president had chosen more than two terms. But he made himself as comfortable as possible, given his debility, in his own peculiar ways. In his private bedroom, his bed was a small, narrow white iron bedstead with a thin mattress and a gray shawl at the foot, under a plain seersucker spread. He kept a gray sweater close, to wear over his night clothes when he had a cold. Nearby stood a white painted table with a towel hung over it, a few books including a prayer book, a package of cigarettes, nose drops, aspirin, and pieces of paper with phone numbers on them. On the wall were photos of his children, and over a door at one end of the room was the tail of a horse raised by his father. Perhaps no other world leader slept in such modest circumstances (although like him, others might have slipped from time to time into a nearby bedroom where a willing companion awaited).

His evenings, when not full of work or playing poker with a circle of friends, were largely his own. He loved to mix drinks for guests, especially Manhattans (proudly squeezing the oranges himself), but he loved even more being by himself, reading, making new additions to his stamp collection, and playing solitaire. He had much to ponder.

PROBLEMS AND DIVISIONS

In most ways, the "First New Deal," 1933-35, was not much of a success. Despite the social programs enacted, Roosevelt himself had also urged a balanced budget, making rapid improvements impossible. Congressional conservatives resisted his appeals for more money, although progressive Republicans from the Midwest and Plains states pushed his legislation forward, and Southern Democrats looked to the White House for the economic salvation of their farmers. Roosevelt's early efforts did not fully meet the crisis overwhelming the nation or respond adequately to the sense of outrage at misunderstood efforts.

At the root of the problem was not only the ongoing collapse of the economy but also a fundamental division of views within the Administration. Harold Ickes, directing the Public Works Division of the Department of the Interior, treated his office as if he were a corporate employer seeking to get the most value for his capital and preferred offering funds for equipment rather than workers. Harry Hopkins, a near-socialist as social worker, believed, by contrast, that putting people to work had its own benefit, giving them the opportunity to earn and then spend. Sending mixed messages, the New Deal sometimes acted against itself.

Farm policies offer the best example of missteps and misunderstanding. Roosevelt told his radio audience in the fourth Fireside Chat, October 22, 1933, that in the "edifice of recovery…dedicated to and maintained for a greater social justice," the production of commodities would need to be restricted for a time, in order to raise prices. The new Agricultural Adjustment Administration (AAA) proposals won the confidence and cooperation of Southern cotton farmers, Western white farmers and Southeast tobacco farmers and would soon win similar cooperation from corn-hog farmers in the Midwest. By curtailing production, the government could regulate prices, and farmers would meanwhile be rewarded for their part in the bargain.

Before good effects could be felt, however, cotton had been planted, and pigs already born. All this had to be destroyed (although the resulting pork was distributed to families on relief). The consequences of "plowing under" needed crops renewed an old question long ignored by businessmen and mainstream politicians. Was the real worth of human sweat gathering the earth's bounty the value that it had for human use, or was it merely the purposes of private profit? If Franklin Roosevelt of 1933-34 had aimed at engineering broad changes in the nature of the social system, crop expansion for social needs would have made more sense. But it might also have upset market calculations. The New Deal was meant to promote economic recovery and not intended to be a revolution in economics.

Were farmers themselves helped? Five years after 1932, as a group, they doubled their cash income—but only as a group. Sharecroppers, from the old South all the way west to Missouri, benefited least. Thousands of them, black and white, were actually forced off lands that their families had occupied for generations. Landowners swallowed the profits in government subsidies and restored production by machine, leaving out their former tenants. Still, many farmers large and small did recover.

The soil-conservation program conceived by the New Deal Brains Trust of liberal thinkers and planners marked a different, more lasting kind of success. By 1936, wheat, corn, cotton and tobacco were taken out of production in many places specifically so that farmers would plant crops that enriched rather than depleted the soil. This was a shift that might have inspired a very different, ecological or sustainable model of American agriculture after the New Deal. A continuing growth of mega-farms and agricultural corporations even during the New Deal years pointed, however, toward a more gloomy environmental future.

Recovery for industry was yet more of a challenge, and here, especially, the first New Deal was a distinct failure. Businessmen faced with lower profits or no profits responded by lowering wages to near-starvation levels. The National Industrial Recovery Act did bring public hearings to enable consumers, workers and others to testify on issues of fair application. Employers refused, however, to cooperate or even compromise in circumstances where an absence of labor union organization allowed them complete control. As the crisis continued, the Progress Works Administration underwrote eighty percent of all public construction, an astonishing figure. But only direct action by working people began to rebalance the shape of the industrial reconstruction.

None of Roosevelt's ideas, or those he shared with his Brains Trust, could have succeeded without his ability to restore confidence or at least give hope. His Fireside Chats on the radio had been masterful from the first, convincing millions to stop demanding money that they had invested in banks and actually put savings back into the vaults. In a brilliant turn of a phrase based upon Jesus' action against the priests of old, he declared that "the money changers...fled from their high seats in the temple." He would return them rather than, as many hoped, replace them with government ownership. But at least the bankers returned with new legislative restraints. More important, they bore the weight, for the rest of the Depression, of public scrutiny and skepticism. They were no longer seen as lords of finance to be worshipped, larger than life figures who magically produced goods and profits.

Reconstruction, Roosevelt-style, demanded something different. "I have continued to recognize three related steps," he pronounced in a Fireside Chat on June 28, 1934. "The first was relief because the primary concern of any government dominated by the humane ideals of democracy is the simple principle that in a land of vast resources no one should be permitted to starve." This was, in reality, a doctrine shockingly new for the American presidency. Neither the Founding Fathers nor Abraham Lincoln or the twentieth century liberals before Roosevelt (certainly not Woodrow Wilson, often credited with laying the groundwork for the New Deal) had put any such principle into action. Relief for the poor had traditionally been the bailiwick of the states, counties and local governments; Herbert Hoover's relief program had been for business and banks mainly.

Historians were later to credit the social movement from the bottom for bringing Roosevelt's best instincts to the fore and giving his vision the challenge as well as the needed political backing for success. And with good reason: something was happening.

AMERICANS GET RADICAL

Conservatives predictably blamed Communist influences. Actually, Communist success had been fairly limited at the bottom of the Depression. But by the time Roosevelt entered office, and increasingly over the course of 1933-34, the restlessness of the unemployed had prompted the formation of powerful relief organizations, Communist-led and otherwise, which held conventions and staged peaceful marches, demanding relief. Roosevelt advisor Harry Hopkins, former president of the American Association of Social Workers, swiftly created a network of trained staff members, replacing the political appointees who had led most local relief agencies, and set out to solve problems. Conditions remained desperate to the point of hopelessness, especially among nonwhite populations and for many in slums and in rural areas. But with modest improvements, an expectation of further improvements blossomed, and in the slightly longer run, the adulation of Roosevelt.

Here, the most puzzling as well as the most dynamic qualities of Roosevelt were simultaneously on display. Frances Perkins, his labor secretary, reflected that he was "the most complicated human being I have ever known." Eleanor Roosevelt called it an "innate kind of reticence" about revealing himself or his plans. No one, neither conservatives, liberals or radicals, could accurately accuse him of having anything like a precise philosophy of governing. At first, it was difficult to see how he might succeed.

There were pragmatic reasons for Roosevelt to act both swiftly and carefully. The early Depression years, closest in American history to the impoverished 1870s (a time when "bread riots" broke out widely and revolutionaries took over St. Louis),led to radical mobilizations that challenged the existing social system, and then, amazingly, became part of a rapidly changing system. Franklin Roosevelt and some of his advisors and functionaries entered into an informal and complicated relationship with Communists, socialists and other radicals. Their ranks included the labor organizers, artists and writers who had the energies and creative powers to develop a new working plan for advanced democracy across the board, from economics to politics and culture. This relationship was still more complicated because admitting that his administration worked with Communists, in particular, would have given Republicans and Democratic conservatives more weapons to use against New Deal programs.

The process began in the last few years of Hoover's term, at the local level especially. Radical demands on behalf of desperate citizens sometimes moved sympathetic city officials to respond positively rather than using force against demonstrators. Meanwhile, radicals themselves began to develop strategic sophistication, including the advantage of working with local allies who had but no particular political views but did have charisma and a public following.

Thus, the Unemployed Councils, led by the Communist Party, had turned from violent confrontations with local police in 1929-30 to a more practical effort to secure food and shelter for the worst hit populations. The Workers Alliance, led by Socialists, adopted a similar strategy. In Harlem, where neighborhood Communists learned to work with the charismatic minister Father Divine, they achieved great popularity. Elsewhere, they negotiated with authorities, often hiding their Communist credentials (to the satisfaction of the officials, who usually knew quite well but chose not to admit their associations). Toward 1933-35, some radicals working among the poor also chose an "American approach" with patriotic symbols and slogans, while urging self-help, mainly the cooperative growing and harvesting of crops in unoccupied fields, as a way to get through the worst of times.

By 1933, troubled Americans in practically all walks of life looked to the federal government for relief. The founding of the Workers Alliance of America in 1935, formed out of several existing groups of unemployed, pushed influential sections of the unemployed organizers towards lobbying Congress. As their importance was eclipsed, the unemployed movement's participants could look back at having refuted the popular conservative ideas that unemployed people were responsible for their own condition, and that relief practices amounted to the jobless sponging funds from the taxpayer. Poverty had not vanished by any means, but the movement's particular contribution was complete.

The Roosevelt Administration itself shifted toward reaching out to representatives of the poor. Those representatives reached back, and not only because they found themselves increasingly acceptable. In 1934, responding to the victory of Hitler in Germany, Georgi Dimitrov, leader of the Bulgarian Communist Party and a major figure in the Communist International, proclaimed the necessity of a global "Popular Front Against Fascism." No longer looking toward the overthrow of corporate capitalism anywhere in the short run, he articulated the new Russian view, quickly adopted by Communists everywhere, of working with socialists, liberals and others in common cause. Resistance to the fascist threat encouraged a wide series of reform activities to make life better in small ways. Across the parts of Europe that had not fallen to fascism already, Communist movements now grew rapidly, influencing non-communist governments and being influenced by them in turn.

A microcosm of that change also happened to the "rent strike" movement. Especially in New York City but a little later in other cities, local government rent boards began negotiations between tenants and landlords, mediating the worst of disputes and seeking to keep people in their apartments or homes. The most energetic of rent strike organizers often became active members of these rent boards: they understood the

William Gropper

situation best, and knew they needed to work out compromises in order to make best use of the local political dynamics. Especially but not only among ethnic groups where Communists had a foothold—Jews, Greeks, Finns, Hungarians, Lithuanians, Armenians and assorted Slavs but also small populations such as Bulgarians—they came to be seen as responsible and responsive neighborhood leaders.

FARM HOLIDAYS AND GENERAL STRIKES

The Farm Holiday movement, seeking to reduce output especially among milk producers in the Midwest and Plains states, reached out to the Roosevelt Administration with appeals and political threats. Influenced by Communists mainly in the northern Midwest, among Finnish-American communities, and across parts of Minnesota where Finns, Norwegians and others supported the Farmer Labor Party, it reached Iowa and Nebraska briefly in 1933-34, rousing particular fears of votes in the 1936 presidential elections not far ahead. Roosevelt, who had special feelings for farm populations ever since his first political campaigns in New York State, was eager to accommodate farmers, while reluctant to alienate commodity corporations and assorted middle men who were blamed for squeezing profits out of low payments for farm products.

The labor movement was another story, one many would say became the most important development in Roosevelt's re-election. Unions had almost collapsed with the Depression. But they began to come roaring back with the first small, but significant waves of a drive for industrial unions, encompassing all workers in a factory or workplace. At great personal risk, low-paid organizers in Detroit, among auto workers still employed, elsewhere among steelworkers, textile workers and others, talked quietly about the need and potential of an all-inclusive unionization. The exclusionary American Federation of Labor, barely holding on, still showed little interest in unskilled workers, and outright hostility toward Communists and other radicals threatening to become successful.

The outbreak of general strikes or near-general strikes in three American cities during 1934 offered still more evidence that things had to change and might change peacefully. The most dramatic was certainly in San Francisco during the final two weeks of July. Seamen and warehouse workers' unions that had been destroyed by repression during the 1920s came back to life with a suddenness when unions demanded their own control of hiring halls (in place of the notorious practice of "shaping up" daily, in which the price of a day's work went to the bottom of the scale). A resulting confrontation led to massive picket lines at the docks, and to the police killing of two union men on July 5, 1934. Almost spontaneously but following careful mobilization of the blue-collar public at large, a funeral march of 20,000 stunned the city fathers (many of whom headed for the hills of Oakland, sure that the "Revolution" had arrived), and 130,000 striking workers essentially shut the city down. At the end, the dockworkers' demands were met and the stage set for widespread unionization of all sea trades and a popular leftwing, often militantly anti-racist mood in the Bay Area for decades to come. Communist leaders of the strikes quickly assumed a responsible role in negotiating with ship owners' associations.

The Minneapolis Teamster strike of the same year was almost as dramatic and important in its consequences. From February to May, 1934, strikes moved from industry to industry, unionists fighting police in the bitter cold. Finally, twenty thousand strikers and sympathizers occupied a central marketplace, broadcasting live on a local radio station they had taken over, peacefully, for a little while. Once again, on July 20, after police fired on unarmed pickets, crowds turned out. This time, 100,000 appeared at the funeral of a striker. Of greatest importance to Roosevelt, Minnesota governor Floyd Olson ordered a halt to all truck transportation into the Twin Cities if a settlement were not reached. The truck fleet owners gave in. The success of unionization here as elsewhere remained limited in many ways, but the backbone of employer resistance to union contracts had been broken. Minneapolis-St Paul, like the Bay Area of San Francisco, Berkeley and Oakland, was a union zone.

Across the South and through parts of New England, workers (many of them women, and in the South, children) in the textile industry staged an almost industry-wide general strike. In the little state of Rhode Island, most dramatically, National Guardsmen fired upon strikers, killing several, prompting reform-minded governor Theodore Francis Green to declare a state emergency and lay out conditions for return to normal. All known Communists in the state were briefly arrested (most of them were small businessmen or teenagers, hardly involved in the strikes), while corporate management was informed that unionization was now legal and union members would be protected hereafter by law. Green, a strong supporter of Roosevelt and the father of "Little New Deal" legislation in the state, had neatly solved a political dilemma and made Rhode Island safely Democratic for generations to come. Elsewhere, arrangements would be complicated in other ways, but they often followed a similar pattern empowering working class ethnic groups to make gains in government services previously unthinkable.

THE PRESIDENT AND HIS ENEMIES

Roosevelt became a hero more and more to ordinary people, as much because of his enemies as because of his own acts. The Supreme Court, seeking a case to test the constitutionality of the National Industrial Recovery Act and the National Recovery Administration, pounced upon the "sick chicken" case involving the Schecter Poultry Company. Its owners refused to accept government interference in any aspect of their operation, including the presence of fowls that had been unwell before slaughtering. They were successfully convicted, an Appeals Court upheld the conviction, and then the Supreme Court unanimously struck down the poultry code and the NRA administration of the code. This decision confirmed the popular view that conservatives were out to return society to the days of Herbert Hoover, but also that they would use the charge that Roosevelt had centralized power in himself, acting like a dictator. In practical terms, the ruling against the NIRA meant chaos for much of American commerce. On the same day, the Supreme Court, in another unanimous vote, wiped out the New Deal program making loans available to mortgage-stretched farmers, and removed from the president the right to remove a resistant member of the Federal Trade Commission. New Dealers called it "Black Monday." Despite favorable election returns in 1934, Roosevelt seemed stymied.

Thus developments had reached a new phase by 1934-35, such that popular movements began to openly defend the New Deal gains and the Roosevelt program against conservative resistance. The President had encouraged this popular support through rhetoric that was, by the standards of only a few years earlier, almost subversive. He had actually come into line with the platforms and rhetoric of the Progressives running Wisconsin and the Farmer-Laborites in next-door Minnesota.

These programs were more popular among ordinary people than could easily be imagined because most newspapers, radio stations and other sources of information remained in corporate hands, not changed much by the effects of the Depression. Ordinary people increasingly supported the New Deal and many began to revere Roosevelt because the realities of unemployment cut into myths about the land of plenty for all willing to work, and because New Deal programs were beginning to work. When federal relief officials responded to conservatives by cutting back programs, first limiting hours (thus lowering pay) and then eliminating jobs entirely, protesters gathered in a dozen cities for demonstrations, and tens of thousands wrote their congressmen.

EUROPE IN CRISIS

A Supreme Court ruling against a major portion of the NIRA in May, 1935, effectively ended the "First New Deal," but Roosevelt had created the constituency necessary to support him onward. Unfortunately, he also had other problems to worry about. The global situation was rapidly changing for the worse in many different if connected ways. Italy had fallen to Fascism in 1923 when Mussolini seized power, and if the sympathetic response of many American businessmen toward the dictatorship remained largely unmoved by reports of repression, liber-

als and the anti-fascist wing of the Italian-American community publicized the reports of ominous prospects. As fascists consolidated their influence in Hungary and pro-Nazi organizations appeared across Europe, Fascism became a pattern rather than a mere symptom of trouble. With the rise of Hitler in Germany in 1933, it had become a threat to society worldwide.

The roots of a possible or partial solution had already been set down during the 1920s. It was not a solution for real global cooperation, but a rational, corporate version of cooperation with common business goals. There the problem remained and grew worse, as Japan's appetite for expansion also brought bloody results in Asia.

Herbert Hoover, the former Secretary of Commerce who assumed the presidency in 1928, had argued for a "greater mutuality of interest" around the globe under U.S. direction. Social stability, world peace, and expansion of trade could dampen conflicts of all kinds, including labor-management differences that had spurred the global movements of socialists and communists then threatening to overtake a war-shattered capitalism from Europe to Asia. As president, Hoover transformed the Department of Commerce from a national regulatory agency to an agency with a global purview, especially regarding markets, loans and the use of natural resources. Revolutions of every kind were to be prevented, private property to be protected, and the property of U.S. corporations and individuals to be protected above all. The Russian influence would therefore be contained, the nationalistic and threatening Germany and Japan cajoled into cooperation, and Britain persuaded that its own version of world leadership had now been bypassed by Washington.

The contradictions within this plan had begun to unravel before Roosevelt took office. Thomas Lamont, a leading American banker, was actually financing Japan's territorial ambitions and economic penetration of the Asian mainland, even as the Japanese army raced across the Manchurian peninsula. Government plans to finance railway and communications systems within China were vetoed by Wall Street, convinced that the Japanese were sure military winners and would be long-run partners of American business. When the League of Nations condemned the Japanese action, Japan promptly withdrew. Any idea of a world community, even a world community guided by business interests, was nearing a state of collapse. From a business standpoint, many American leaders approached the conclusion that only war could protect investments abroad.

Americans' early opinions of Adolf Hitler had at first been to ridicule his rise to power in Germany. A little man with a big mustache prone to shouting, he seemed as ridiculous as comics like Charlie Chaplin and the Three Stooges were to make him look in movies. Among population groups, some German-Americans showed sympathy for the Fuehrer, while Italian-American supporters of Mussolini grew convinced that their homeland dictator also had more support. But the most valuable of Hitler's American supporters came, for several years after 1933, from the wealthy and powerful classes. Fearing Communism would triumph worldwide thanks to miserable conditions, leading American newspapers, important political figures and sources of educated opinion greeted the new Chancellor with sympathy or indifference. How could Hitler, who insisted that he would defend private property and religion, be a worse threat than Communists? He would, they believed, certainly protect American assets in Germany, a significant plus for General Electric among other corporations and bankers. The greater worries of American investment bankers and other elites toward Hitler and Mussolini had a different character. During the late 1890s, President William McKinley began to use the phrase "Open Door" to explain American demands upon other nations and their colonies. By this policy, all the world should be open to U.S. exports on fair, favorable conditions; those who refused for national reasons to do so were inviting conflict. On the other hand, the U.S. retained the right to limit imports as suited national interest. Much of American foreign policy would be guided by this curious imbalance, and by a political corollary: because the U.S. was a leading moral force in the world, it had the right to enforce its demands. The imbalance was greater in respect to the Western Hemisphere, and had been so since President James Monroe's Secretary of State John Quincy Adams had formulated what became as the "Monroe Doctrine" in the early 1820s. It stated that any future European colonialist ventures or interference in the Americas would be viewed as aggressive acts requiring a U.S. response. No other nation could interfere with US prerogatives, not even residents of those nations, from the Mexican border southward to the Pole. This policy, explained as a measure to protect our southern neighbors, clearly had other purposes.

Sylvia Wald

Easter Shopping

THE GHOST OF THE MONROE DOCTRINE

Roosevelt himself seemed to send contradictory messages to the rest of the Western Hemisphere. Administrations just previous to Roosevelt's had begun a reassessment of traditional U.S. policies in Latin America. Long marked by armed interventions to protect corporate investments, these moves had become known as "Gunboat Diplomacy," and some business leaders themselves argued for a less confrontational strategy, applying economic pressures to achieve the same ends. The long-planned replacement of British economic and political influence with U.S. influence in the Caribbean added more reasons to adjust policies and, especially, the diplomatic rhetoric.

The "Good Neighbor Policy" formulated by Hoover and continued under Roosevelt was a sideways step from the century-old Monroe Doctrine. In one of several Pan-American conferences, he joined others in pledging that no country would interfere in the "internal or external affairs" of any of the others in the Hemisphere. Still, in 1933, Roosevelt responded to a revolution in Cuba against an unpopular dictatorship by sending U.S. warships to circle the island. He refused to recognize the new, moderately left-of-center government, and after a military coup went on to establish close ties with the repressive government of Fulgencio Batista, notably friendly to American business interests. New loans were arranged, and the U.S. abrogated the Platt Amendment (dating to the Spanish-American War and allowing Americans to control Cuban affairs) in return for rights to remain in control of the Guantanamo naval base.

This treatment of Cuba could be seen as "good-neighborly" because the U.S. had restrained itself from actual military occupation. Roosevelt likewise ended the U.S. military occupation of Haiti and Nicaragua, long protecting the powerful classes against the poor. Likewise, direct U.S. overlordship of the little nation of Panama, site of the Panama Canal in territory taken from Colombia, was eased somewhat if not ended. Still, investment banker and future Central Intelligence Agency director Allen Dulles privately made it clear that no Good Neighbor Policy would deter the U.S. from intervention in the region, when and where it chose to do so.

Another historically unwilling partner, in a different ocean neighboring the U.S., also faced a curious liberation. The successful conquest of the Philippines, causing starvation and the deaths of hundreds of thousands of Filipinos (some historians later called this the prelude to the U.S. invasion of Vietnam), had kept U.S. forces in place there since the late 1890s. In 1934, under pressure both from the AFL to eliminate potential labor competition from Filipino immigrants and from military officials who warned that Americans could not easily protect their Pacific colony from a widely-expected Japanese invasion, the Tydings-McDuffie Act declared the nation would become truly independent in twelve years (that is, 1946). Overpowering U.S. influence was not expected to end, however.

EUROPEAN DEBTS

Europeans felt the ambiguities in these policies as well. Offering little help to countries deeply in debt, Hoover had urged them to cooperate economically and to continue the process of disarmament begun during the 1920s. He hoped, he insisted, to rid the world of offensive weapons. Europeans outside of Italy and Germany, fearful of a future invasion, were pessimistic, all the more because the conclusion of the First World War had left the U.S. as the one military powerhouse on the planet, perhaps benign, perhaps not so benign. As so often in the rest of the twentieth century and beyond, U.S. leaders seemed to be urging others to lay down their arms and to trust that Washington would do what was best for all.

Similarly, Roosevelt declined to agree with European leaders on an economic stabilization plan or any plan at all that might limit American flexibility to recover in its own way, whatever the effect on others. At the time of the prestigious London Conference sponsored by the League of Nations in 1934, Roosevelt suggested to Raymond Moley that he tell the Europeans "what our American recovery program is doing to raise prices, relieve debtors and increase purchasing power," and if Europeans did not agree, "then there's nothing to cooperate about." The U.S. would, on principal, make none of the formal concessions the Europeans wanted, chief among them stabilizing exchange rates of currency at a time when the American economy was gaining from the continuing fall in value of the dollar (making American manufactures and produce cheaper to foreign markets). The "Open Door" remained unchanged under the new president. Americans seemed to have promised more than they delivered in offering to lead salvation through stability.

Chapter Three

THE 1934 MIDTERM ELECTIONS GAVE THE DEMOCRATS AN EVEN GREATER MAJORITY IN CONGRESS.

AFTER THAT, FDR WORRIED LESS ABOUT HIS ENEMIES ON THE RIGHT THAN THE LEFT.

THERE IS NO EXCUSE FOR POVERTY IN A STATE AS RICH AS CALIFORNIA!

UPTON SINCLAIR

THE MUCKRAKING WRITER AND FORMER SOCIALIST RAN FOR GOVERNOR AS A DEMOCRAT.

HE SWEPT THE PRIMARIES WITH HIS E.P.I.C. PLAN.

END POVERTY IN CALIFORNIA!

$50 A MONTH PENSIONS FOR POOR PEOPLE OVER AGE 60.

WE'D BETTER MOVE AHEAD WITH SOCIAL SECURITY.

SINCLAIR WAS DEFEATED WITH A DELUGE OF SPENDING BY THE HOLLYWOOD STUDIOS.

SENATOR HUEY LONG OF LOUISIANA WENT EVEN FURTHER.

EVERY MAN A KING

SHARE OUR WEALTH

HE WAS POPULAR, RUTHLESS AND RUNNING FOR PRESIDENT.

HE'LL STEAL YOUR VOTES.

WE'LL STEAL HIS THUNDER.

LONG WAS STOPPED BY AN ASSASSIN'S BULLET, BUT HIS AGENDA INFLUENCED THE 2nd NEW DEAL.

MILITANT LABOR WAS ENCOURAGED BY THE

NATIONAL INDUSTRIAL RECOVERY ACT

WHICH RECOGNIZED THE RIGHT TO ORGANIZE UNIONS.

IN SAN FRANCISCO, THE 1934 LONGSHOREMENS' STRIKE PARALYZED THE LARGEST PORT ON THE WEST COAST.

DON'T SCAB

EMPLOYERS RESPONDED WITH REPLACEMENT WORKERS AND VIOLENCE.

TWO MEN WERE SHOT DEAD BY POLICE ON JULY 5th, "BLOODY THURSDAY."

RIOTS ERUPTED AND THE GOVERNOR CALLED IN THE NATIONAL GUARD.

DOZENS OF UNIONS VOTED TO STRIKE IN SUPPORT, AND THOUSANDS JOINED IN.

THE GENERAL STRIKE SHUT THE CITY DOWN.

THE COUNTRY SEEMS POISED FOR REVOLT.

The Turning Point

OPPOSITION TO THE NEW DEAL–
FROM THE GRASS ROOTS OF AMERICA'S COUNTRY CLUBS

The New Deal reached a definite turning point as the elections of 1936 approached, casting Roosevelt's main achievements in doubt but also rallying supporters. He had first been elected because the country fell into crisis and because the Democratic machine delivered votes. This time, the political landscape looked very different.

The New Deal set loose electoral forces far beyond those previously experienced by Roosevelt—forces both for and against him. In the process, it began to realign much of the country along liberal/progressive versus conservative/reactionary lines more than the traditional two-party method of dividing power and benefits among regional elites and religious or ethnic groups. But its success also tended to associate progress with "big government," while squeezing out traditional opponents of all kinds to conscription and to military commitments abroad.

New Dealers joked that opposition to Roosevelt seemed to be springing up from the grass roots of country clubs all across the privileged classes of America. *The Literary Digest*, a popular weekly, predicted from its own polling that the Republican candidate, former Kansas governor Alfred Landon, would sweep away the president and his Democratic majority in Congress, revealing both as a mere passing phenomenon of the economic crisis. Behind Landon stood powerful groups of business interests charging that Roosevelt was eroding property rights and creating a socialist (or even Soviet-style) America.

Not only Republicans felt this way. Former Roosevelt ally and more recent Democratic rival Al Smith joined Wall Street financier John Raskob in the ultra-conservative American Liberty League. Smith told a banquet of ultra-wealthy listeners in early 1936 that the president was rousing one class (the poor) against another (those in the room). FDR's advisors were, he hinted, disguised versions of Karl Marx and V.I. Lenin, perhaps even supporters of the "godless Union of the Soviets." Meanwhile, lower class right wingers like the Silver Shirts, newborn counterparts to the Ku Klux Klan, and similar groups held anti-Roosevelt, anti-union, aggressively racist rallies in many cities, raising anxieties about a possible American fascism calling itself "Americanism."

Roosevelt had greater political strength than his enemies imagined. But he had to consolidate that strength by borrowing further ideas and energies from political movements on the Left, and he badly needed an energized labor movement to mobilize voter enthusiasm. Help came in unexpected packages.

In California, famed socialistic novelist Upton Sinclair developed a cooperative platform that he called EPIC (*i.e.*, End Poverty In California) and wrote a best-selling book about what he would do if elected governor. He narrowly missed being elected in 1934 as a dissident Democrat running strongly against the party machine for the nomination, but was defeated in the general election by an all-out state conservative push. In his efforts, he brought tens of thousands of reform-minded Californians into active politics.

Similarly, Norman Thomas, the Socialist Party candidate of 1932 who personally continued a dramatic campaign for human rights, had created a voting machine for social change—but not for himself. When asked if (as conservatives charged) Roosevelt had carried out the Socialist platform of 1932, he quipped that it had actually been carried "out on a stretcher," badly injured if not dead to the world. Thomas's own voters disagreed, many of them moving into state-based third parties that supported the president in 1936 or into reform-minded sections of the Democratic Party. Sinclair, Thomas and others outside the two-party system had actually helped move the New Deal leftward, and to attract the popular constituencies that radicals and reformers had done so much to build.

POPULISM, THE REAL (KING FISH) THING

Roosevelt nearly faced another and possibly more dangerous opponent: Louisiana governor Huey P. Long, known far and wide as "the Kingfish." Son of the leader of the state's once-powerful Socialist Party, Long had been elected in 1928 as governor, and he proceeded to improve roads, education, medical care and schools; unlike other Southern Democrats, he did not run promising to "protect" whites against African-Americans. He also ruled with an iron hand, fixing elections when necessary, and otherwise acting like a Southern Democrat in office. Elected Senator in 1930, he created a national "Share the Wealth" movement, promising to take away money from the rich and give it to the poor under the slogan "Every man a king." With his charges that the Democrats and Republicans supported the same class of rich people, and his folksy appeal to ordinary Americans feeling disempowered, he gained millions of followers.

Long seemed, for a while, to ally himself with Dr. Francis Townsend, an elderly pensions reformer in California, and with the demagogic Father Charles Coughlin, popular radio priest who railed against bankers and Jews with equal vigor. Only Long's assassination in 1935 prevented a powerful third-party presidential campaign that might have robbed Roosevelt of decisive votes and thrown the election to Landon. The resulting Liberty Bell Party, more conservative than populist, failed to attract voters or even much interest. Unlike Norman Thomas, who ran again in 1936 but gained far fewer votes than before, Communists themselves ran a curious sort of shadow slate for president, spending most of their efforts attacking the Republicans and indirectly supporting FDR.

THE DEMAGOG   Gus Peck

Meanwhile, Roosevelt had been working hard to win back the support of farmers, workers, the aged and the unemployed. In April, 1935, he managed to get legislation enacted for the Emergency Relief Appropriation Act, and along with it the Social Security Act. Three months later, the National Labor Relations Act, informally titled the "Wagner Act" for New York senator Robert F. Wagner, went into law.

Emergency Relief offered only temporary employment, Social Security offered only tiny payments to begin with and the National Labor Relations Act only guaranteed the right for labor to organize, not guaranteeing unionism protection from business strategies to prevent it. Nonetheless, taken together these represented a significant step in a new progressive direction, one not unnoticed by the public.

LABOR'S GIANT STEP

The response of labor was in many ways the most dramatic event of 1935. During the previous year, the two city general strikes in San Francisco and Minneapolis-St. Paul had both shaken business leaders and given working people a sense of self-confidence in collective action. In 1935, at the convention of the conservative American Federation of Labor, coal miners' leader John L. Lewis answered a personal insult by socking a fellow labor bureaucrat in the jaw. Lewis and a half-dozen other union leaders then stormed out of the meeting. They had demanded the right to organize industrial unions, that is, not merely encompassing the skilled and privileged workers in the standard AFL method, but all who toiled together in any workplace. Now, joined by thousands of enthusiastic volunteers, they were going to seize that right for themselves. Eight unions, soon joined by two others, formed the Committee for Industrial Organization (CIO). In 1938, the CIO became the Congress of Industrial Organizations, a true rival federation to the AFL.

Furious campaigns for unionization of autoworkers, steel workers and rubber workers among others now began, frequently with radicals of various kinds doing the most dangerous organizing. Labor activists cornered by hired gangs and sometimes by local police "red squads" (formed earlier to contain a supposed Socialist or Communist threat) were beaten badly on many occasions, arrested or driven from towns. Labor organizers found support and rooms for meetings among secular ethnic organizations that had built up clubhouses in the 1910s-20s in blue collar districts and offered cultural activities as well as benefits to the sick and funerals for dead members. Here, older and younger generations met to realize dreams of industrial democracy unfulfilled for generations.

CIO leaders and new members naturally faced the ire of the AFL, which considered the group not only a rival but an enemy out to ruin organized labor's reputation for respectability. Miners' leader John L. Lewis nevertheless became a virtual god to hundreds of thousands of workers as he devoted miners' funds and organizing expertise to the Steel Workers Organizing Committee, defying all the rules of the AFL for separate craft organization. It was no secret that Lewis, personally a Republican but always a shrewd tactician, invited Communists to the table. His intimate advisor, Communist supporter Lee Pressman, was made the general legal counsel of the CIO, and tough Communist organizers quickly made their way upward into leadership in many places. Here, the National Labor Relations Act and its creation, the National Labor Relations Board, proved crucial. Organizers proclaimed that "the president wants you to join a union," a stretch but not too much of a stretch, with an election ahead.

The mobilization of CIO union members and sympathizers for 1936 was the beginning of a love-match between Roosevelt and the dynamic section of labor, each side needing the other badly. In the summer before the election, John L. Lewis personally launched Labor's Non-Partisan League (LNPL), making a massive mobilization of labor votes for FDR possible. Many local unionists reluctantly gave up their dream of a revived Socialist party or better, a national labor party. Roosevelt became their cause.

The role of radicals within the labor movement working furiously for Roosevelt's re-election drove conservatives wild, but also marked one of the most amazing turnarounds in the history of American social movements.

THE PECULIARITY OF AMERICAN REFORM

Some New Deal aims at recovery had a unique American quality. No other large nation on earth has had such a high proportion of home owners or has defined prosperity in terms of proportions of home owners. Most unusual, in some ways, has been home ownership by blue collar workers and their families. This phenomenon was clearly visible as early as the 1910s in some big city neighborhoods but especially in small cities and towns, along with farm homesteads, thanks in part to the efficiency of home-builders and eagerness of Americans to live in even the smallest of individual dwellings rather than continuing to rent.

The Depression slowed down home-buying and home-building to a dead crawl. In 1932, just before FDR took office, a quarter million mortgages were "written off" each month, and three million families lost their homes, despite partial payment on their mortgages. The First New Deal moved on the problem with two new agencies: the Home Owners Loan Corporation (HOLC), brought into existence by Congress in June 1933, and the Federal Housing Administration

(FHA), the next year. Like the Veterans Administration, created in 1930, the FHA was destined for a long life, influential in the lives of millions of homes and tens of millions of prospective buyers.

The recovery of housing exceeded the recovery of the economy in general. From fewer than 100,000 housing starts in 1933, the number climbed to more than 300,000 four years later and 600,000 by 1941. HOLC had the unique role of refinancing mortgages in trouble. In its first two years, it made loans of more than $3 billion for a million mortgages, an astonishing tenth of all those in the U.S. that year. The role of the FHA was to reassure and reimburse the creditor. Together, they made possible down payments for no more than 7% of the value of a house and lengthened the time limit on repayment.

There was a distinct down side, several times over. First, the opportunity to create more livable cities based upon regional economies, with environmentally-sound transportation policies rather than increased reliance upon family-owned vehicles, was abandoned (see Chapter Five). Much potential park space in and around cities vanished for private profit. Second, the return of housing growth coincided with racial and residential discrimination, another example of the ways in which the New Deal benefited white working (or poor) people, lifting them out of poverty and increasing the social and cultural distance from the great majority of nonwhites, not only African-Americans. The HOLC and FHA based their systems of assistance on such criteria as racial "homogeneity" of neighborhoods and their prosperity or poverty (thus refusing funds to the "declining" city neighborhoods where nonwhites would most likely be moving). FHA officials, wary of lost property values for their agencies, actually insisted upon racial covenants barring nonwhites from "white" zones of residence (a rule made illegal only in 1948, by a Supreme Court ruling).

The United States became a land of many homeowners, but this

C. Crosby Allen

"Well, boys, what's unconstitutional today?"

landscape was racially divided, with millions of nonwhites unable to obtain mortgages even if they had the resources for a down payment. Communists, Socialists and small numbers of liberals drew resentment, hostility and sometimes violent reprisals for seeking to break down residential segregation. That task, growing more difficult with accelerated suburbanization, remained a burden upon future generations to solve—or face the consequences.

HENRY WALLACE, THE FARMERS' MAN

In much of Europe and the rest of the world, the working population of the cities and a scattering of intellectuals, small businessmen and others drove society forward. Rural populations were considered backward, tied to traditional habits (and religious beliefs), unwilling to change. Populism, the American political and economic movement of the 1880s-90s, had been different, sometimes more deeply interracial than any other in the country, built from the creation of farm marketing cooperatives. People's Party candidates had been kept out of office through fraud and violence, especially in the South, and the party's remaining energy absorbed into the Democratic Party of William Jennings Bryan, its frequent candidate for president. But even as the rural population grew dramatically smaller, something of the radical legacy survived and took new shape.

Among the strongest and also strangest of personalities within the New Deal administrative leaders was Secretary of Agriculture, Henry Agard Wallace. His grandfather, trained as a minister, founded *Wallace's Farmer*, an influential journal dedicated to defending farm life and improving it through scientific agriculture. Henry's father joined the Harding Administration as Secretary of Agriculture, turning the journal over to the third generation. "H.A." inherited a passion for modernized farming, studying genetics, statistics and agricultural sciences, while insisting that the nation's most hard-hit family farmers needed federal funds to achieve stable incomes. Henry Wallace added to his growing fame with strong, eclectic religious views that he shared on occasion with the public in the years after he taught an adult Sunday School class in Iowa.

The Wallaces had been a Republican family, and in 1933 Henry was one of two Republicans appointed to the Cabinet—taking his father's old job. He worked hard to restore prosperity to the quarter of the American people who still lived in rural areas, and while devoting energy to the previously successful farmer, increasingly turned toward rural (and urban) poverty with programs of food stamps and school lunches. Determined to use scientific advances for the good of all, he created government programs for land-use planning, erosion control and soil conservation, the use of hybrid seeds and drought-resistant crops. Neither smoker nor drinker, uneasy at the free-wheeling social life of Washington, he called himself a "practical mystic" who sought to bring the inner light of the spirit outward to practical uses. Urban radicals, labor activists, intellectuals and artists hardly knew what to make of Henry Wallace at first. Increasingly, over the course of the 1930s and early 1940s, they came to see him as representing the best of an older America.

THE POPULAR FRONT AGAINST FASCISM

Almost overnight, with the declaration of the Popular Front Against Fascism, American Communists and those considered sympathetic— including many thousands of artists and intellectuals, campus and community activists, and rising labor leaders—gained a new respectability and new degree of influence. Scant years before, some of them had led crowds fighting local police or slugging "scabs" who crossed picket lines. Now they continued to step out into the open as community leaders.

Many reformers not quite identified openly with the Communists made visits to the White House over the next few years, usually at the invitation of Eleanor Roosevelt. They found her sympathetic and she reciprocated. The relationship hinted at a quietly developing trend. Radicals had come to understand the need to abandon near-time revolutionary aspirations. No matter that many still clung to the badly mistaken belief that the USSR had become a model of egalitarian governance and racial or ethnic reconciliation; they had entirely different working plans for the future of a more democratic USA.

The working relationship between the Administration and a host of radicals was further highlighted by Roosevelt's legislative proposals of 1935. Nervous about Huey Long's appeal, FDR was keenly aware that the enactment of Social Security did not address the popular resentment against the rich, and he also felt the sting of the Supreme Court rulings against modest restraints on corporate behavior.

For these reasons among others, Roosevelt dropped a bombshell of several parts. The first part was a progressive inheritance tax, designed to reduce the national debt while shifting wealth from the wealthy classes to those less fortunate. The second part involved a sharp increase on taxes of the wealthy individuals, changing a situation in which those with incomes of over a million dollars were taxed no heavier, proportionally, than if they had made a mere million. The third was directed at corporate profits which, as he pointed out, owed a great deal to assistance in various ways form the government.

FDR knew that these proposals would not reach legislative conclusions before the elections, but he shrewdly stuck a symbolic finger into the eye of the very rich, to the pleasure of an impoverished and outraged public. On the other side of his proposals, he added an assurance to business. The New Deal had "now reached substantial completion," that is to say, the government was unlikely to seek more control over business. The stock market soared in response to the highest level since 1930. Roosevelt was balancing, or juggling, one program against another, and one social class against another. At that kind of juggling, he was nothing short of brilliant.

Roosevelt continued the juggling act on foreign affairs. The Soviet Union, considered by the Catholic church and conservative Protestant denominations as the domain of Satan on earth, actually badly wanted something from Roosevelt that no previous president had granted: diplomatic recognition. Roosevelt cleverly called in the foremost Catholic thinker on global policies, Georgetown University professor Father Edmund Walsh, to discuss the prospects. Walsh later reported that the president had won him over. He would end his personal campaign against recognition of the USSR and urge others to do so as well.

Then Roosevelt turned around to negotiate details with Maxim Litvinov, Soviet foreign minister. American bankers, former Russian aristocrats and others had outstanding claims against Bolshevik seizures of property going back to the 1917 Revolution, and the two men discussed what figure of repayment would satisfy at least some critics. They arrived at $75 million dollars, and Roosevelt considered the deal closed. Roosevelt added, in phrases unimaginable from the

White House previously, "I trust that the relations now established between our peoples may forever remain normal and friendly and that our nations henceforth may cooperation for their mutual benefit and for the preservation of the peace of the world." Not for world peace, as it turned out, but for the defeat of Nazism, this pledge proved crucial to the future of civilization.

ANTIWAR MOODS

Meanwhile, Roosevelt faced a nation whose popular revulsion against war was at a peak. The Nye Committee, named for Congressman Gerald Nye of North Dakota, convened hearings in 1935 about the events leading up to the U.S. declaration of war in 1917. Nye, a progressive Republican, had earlier made his name with hearings about the oil-field corruption of the Harding Administration during the early 1920s, and now seized upon the evidence already known about the military suppliers' lobby urging U.S. entry into the First World War. Evidence against Woodrow Wilson and his banking intimates was damning in the public eye, and the lobbyists for war, with their Wall Street backers, became widely known as "Merchants of Death." No such strong antiwar sentiment would again grip the public until disillusionment with the Vietnam War, a disillusionment that found new form decades later during the U.S. invasion and occupation of Iraq and Afghanistan, the continuing imperial enterprise and its various scandals and miscalculations awakening conservatives as well as liberals and progressives.

On college campuses, students staged strikes, chiefly during 1934-1936, against the flagrant military presence on campus. Students promised to take no part in future wars themselves and adopted slogans like "Build Schools, Not Battleships!" In a few places, notably the University of Wisconsin, progressive college administrators reacted shrewdly, declaring "Peace Days" and shutting down classes willingly for peace rallies on campus. More than half a million students took part in 1936, and the antiwar American Student Union became the largest student organization in U.S. history at the time, before the fear of fascism tamped down the antiwar mood.

The Roosevelt Administration, uneasy with peace movements for a variety of reasons, seemed to turn back to domestic affairs, all the more determined to capture the idealism of the young in particular. The influence of Eleanor Roosevelt became still more evident as the President's second term in office approached. She was famous for saying that if women wanted to be influential in American politics, they would need the "wisdom of the serpent and the guileless appearance of the dove," and that was surely true of herself. If anyone knew what FDR was thinking, she did, or that was the common assumption from newspapermen to well-informed men and women in the street.

THE ELEANOR FACTOR, CONTINUED

Eleanor moved unceasingly to develop different ways to advance her ideas, almost always in advance of Franklin's own in areas of social reform, welfare and racial equality. She pummeled officials of the Administration, high and low, usually in letters asking them to look into some matter, and according to legend, she never forgot that she had asked. Sometimes she visited the particular New Deal agency to demand an appointment and find out why something had not taken place yet, beginning with the formidable phrase, "The President has asked me...." No wonder hostile signs could be found in Republican-leaning stores and barrooms of small towns and country clubs: "We don't like Eleanor, either!"

Her lobbying crossed all political lines in and around the Administration, but she was almost always most influential and friendly among the left-leaning, labor- and minority-supporting administrators. A special outlay of $250,000 funds for milk for the children of Chicago was being held up, for instance, until top federal officials went to see Eleanor and asked her to talk to the President. The funds materialized. In another of many cases, the Christian Socialist minister Sherwood Eddy visited the White House to tell Eleanor about the racist violence ordered by Arkansas landlords against striking tenant farmers. Against the intense objections of Southern Democratic politicians, a Department of Justice investigator was delegated to visit and report back.

Eleanor Roosevelt was also, perhaps naturally, more heavily involved with the Works Progress Administration than almost any other agency. As the 1930s moved onward, the WPA became living proof that a more democratic, more inclusive culture *could* become possible in America, with a recognition of the contributions not only of workers, farmers, children and the poor, but also of African-Americans, Mexican-Americans, Indians and others customarily ignored as non-voters or abused by conservatives but also scarcely defended by many liberals.

She often urged administrators to be more bold and less worried about being accused of "stirring up trouble" locally. She militantly defended Secretary of Labor Frances Perkins from such charges as not arranging the deportation of West Coast longshoremen's union leader and labor idol Harry Bridges, a native of Australia considered dangerously "red" after leading the famed San Francisco General Strike of 1934 and guiding a new configuration of West Coast locals afterward.

Eleanor succeeded most especially in making government more "civil," more open to citizen-led civic groups uncontrolled by business interests. These included the League of Women Voters, the National Association for the Advancement of Colored People, and the National Consumers League, but also groups known more for their political militancy and left leanings, such as the National Sharecroppers Fund, the Workers Alliance, and the American Youth Congress. She fought hard to push through the Wagner Health Act of 1939, considered by the American Medical Association to be "socialized medicine." It could be called the forerunner to the twenty-first century campaign for "single payer" programs, and although de-

feated by powerful forces, it marked an early step in a history of government efforts to improve the nation's health.

Her influence also made a crucial difference in one more respect. More women were employed in high-ranking and middle-ranking positions than ever before in U.S. history. An informal network guided by Eleanor and her friend, Molly Dewson, head of the Women's Division of the Democratic National Committee, found and encouraged the right candidates for available government jobs.

A NEW DEAL FOR INDIANS

Previous federal policies toward Indian tribes, going back to the Dawes Act of the 1880s, had pressed Native populations toward assimilation and loss of language and tribal identity. Behind these policies stood continuing private appropriation of lands with mineral resources, racist treatment by surrounding white communities, and the dwindling of reservation populations to a desperately poor 320,000. In 1924, Congress had given formal citizenship to Indians, but this act improved their situation little. Roosevelt named a former executive secretary of the American Indian Defense Association as the new Commissioner of Indian Affairs in 1933. Commissioner John Collier determined to revive tribal governments and encourage self-determination, prompting Congress to pass the Indian Reorganization Act of 1934. About four million of the 90 million acres stolen since the 1880s were returned to Indian hands. The encouragement to revive Indian culture turned out to be short-lived, ending with the resignation of Collier and the Administration of Harry Truman. But like many New Deal programs, it set a precedent that could be revived at a later time, under more egalitarian leadership.

THE NEW PUBLIC CULTURE

Cultural programs of the New Deal were among the most hated by conservatives—and among the First Lady's favorite efforts to democratize American society in ways that had not been previously been attempted.

The global shift marked by the Popular Front coincided with the Works Progress Administration hiring of thousands of intellectuals and artists, actors, playwrights and historians for a myriad of projects not even on the drawing boards of earlier government-sponsored efforts. Conservative critics complained that the programs were often run by radicals critical of business—and they were correct in this claim. Radical critics, often under their own breath, suggested cynically that intellectuals and artists put to work by the government stopped thinking about revolutionary change—and they were probably right as well.

Whatever the motives for its creation, the Federal Art Project (FAP) marks a high point in democratic imagery and visual representation of New Deal aspirations. Nothing like it had been envisioned before (the creation of the National Endowment for the Arts in 1965 followed the model created under Roosevelt). More than 300,000 artworks were produced in a few years' time, all of them on federal property. By the time Congress cut off funding, ending the project in 1943, ten thousand artists had been employed. Many worked in the arts that Americans could see before their eyes, often on a daily basis. The Federal Art Project notably employed artists to depict local history in murals, most often on public buildings such as post offices. Some of the greatest of contemporary talents, such as Ben Shahn, rushed to the task with a mixture of firm realism, heroization (especially of the hard-working, white male laborers and farmers; women were depicted mostly as home-makers, African-Americans scarcely present) and a stylization that stressed the dignity of work. The Prints division of the FAP, a center for women artists, contributed designs of all kinds, especially for government-sponsored programs and causes such as literacy.

No arts program had more public visibility or controversy than the Federal Theater Project. Its national director, Hallie Flanagan, set out to create real theater for the ordinary American, capturing, in her words, the search "for knowledge about his country and his world, to dramatize his struggle to turn the great, natural, economic and social forces of our time toward a better life for more people." This was achieved, in the four years of the project until shut down by Congress in 1939, through various "units" traveling to localities, cities large and small, with hundreds of plays on various subjects, not only in English but other languages (for immigrants)—comedies, dramas, musicals and dance performances, for adults and children alike.

Shakespeare was the most often performed, but it was the "Living Newspaper" (a sort of oral history of current life), originating in the leftwing Theater of Action, along with Negro theater, that attracted the most hostile congressional attention.

The Federal Writers Project, less controversial with conservatives, accomplished more in a few years than anyone might have imagined. Employing thousands of writers unable to make a living with their craft, it set dozens on the task of surveying their local settings, relating historical details, constructing maps with significant cultural spots, even surveying the games that children played. Other writers, working in the South, interviewed hundreds of former slaves, now in old age, most of them children before emancipation; these interviews, taken down in pencil and pen, remained in archives until edited and published in nearly twenty volumes decades later, a priceless contribution to African-American history made possible by the New Deal.

On the fringes of New Deal programs, a popular appreciation of folk music gathered steam from the middle 1930s, with the gathering of songs and singers by musicologists, and the addition of folksingers white and black to the labor-musical concerts and fundraising events. A Madison Square Garden concert in 1939, "From Spirituals to Swing," dramatized neglected figures like Huddie Ledbetter ("Leadbelly") and honored rising swing musicians with Popular Front credentials. Meanwhile, Woody Guthrie became a beloved figure rhapsodizing his version of American democratic possibilities.

Even Hollywood got in on the act. Among the most fascinating episodes of the time was an adventure film based upon a short story idea by the President himself and titled *The President's Mystery*. Released after the 1936 election, the project had grown out of a promotional drive by *Liberty* magazine early that year, when the editors promised to provide a writer to fill out any plot that FDR devised. In the film, a disillusioned corporate attorney disappears from public sight and turns up in a small town, helping its residents to regain their self-confidence. This may have represented FDR's ideal of a genteel figure who, for all the best reasons, turns against his own inherited class, or the plot may have been concocted by one of his speech-writers. But the idea was a good one in any case, and Republic Studios, eager for a hit, seized on the story, hiring a director and two writers seemingly perfect for the story of a factory town where unemployed farmers and workers resist tyrannical bankers and somehow put the unemployed back to work.

The plot wasn't entirely fanciful. True, the movie invented an adulterous wife for the lawyer to abandon, and an alternative romantic interest for the ex-banker in the little town along with lots of likeable workaday characters. But bankers in real-life America really were shutting down factories, and the mean-spirited swindler seen in the film comported with a widespread public view of financiers. Avoiding anything like a riot or police suppression of sentiment, *The President's Mystery* struck a middle note just as Roosevelt did himself. The film's main screenwriter happened to be Jewish Communist Lester Cole, a driving personal force for the unionization of screenwriters in Hollywood and for mobilization of the public in the campaign against fascism.

If Hollywood in the early 1930s seemed to specialize in gangster films with mobsters taking revenge upon the society that had cheated everyone, the comedy of the day often ridiculed the wealth classes. New Deal-inclined films, some of them with Hollywood's top actors, writers and directors, sparkled from the middle 1930s onward. *Holiday*, starring Cary Grant and Katharine Hepburn, was one of the most famous, about a super-wealthy but terribly bored young woman who had helped workers strike against her father's own business and wanted a way out of her world—with the help of the romantic young man from the lower classes. *Dead End*, developed from a play by Lillian Hellman, depicted life in Manhattan's slums, depicting the desperate poor and an idealistic architect dreaming of a better city, aided by the government. *Grapes of Wrath*, based on John Steinbeck's famous novel, showed dispossessed migrants from Oklahoma to California settled, after much melodrama, into a New Deal-created community. Even *Crime School* (a remake of *Mayor of Hell* starring Jimmy Cagney, released in 1933), a 1938 Warner Brothers film about an uprising of juvenile inmates against a totalitarian prison warden, ended with reformer Humphrey Bogart rushing in, like a New Deal agent, bringing the boys back to order with promises of a new and different kind of treatment and rehabilitation.

MONUMENTS OF THE NEW DEAL

Bridges, dams, and skyscrapers complemented the creation of murals on public buildings during the Roosevelt years. They were, from the standpoint of tourism, often the most visible signs of the New Deal. Sometimes they literally celebrated American life, in pictorial form, as the best on earth; but giant construction projects offered most viewers a similar feeling, that a nation with so much power could accomplish anything, even recovery.

The Hoover Dam, some thirty miles from the then-small town of Las Vegas, had begun construction in 1931, and was completed in less than five years amid often astronomical temperatures. The Grand Coulee Dam in Washington State was higher than Niagara Falls and provided power for much of the Northwest. The Golden Gate Bridge on San Francisco Bay opened to vehicles and pedestrians in 1937. Construction workers died in each of these projects, and from an ecological standpoint, many of the smaller dams built in the same years, including the massive Bonneville Dam, drove fish populations toward extinction and harmed Indian tribes while offering cheap power to corporations fattening their investors' bank accounts. Mount Rushmore's presidential cavalcade of Washington, Jefferson, Lincoln and cousin Theodore Roosevelt, blasted out of the Black Hills sacred to Indians, seemed to many at the time a waste of resources if not a violation. It also proved an instant and lasting tourist attraction.

"Sometimes I wonder why, with all the log cabins there are in America, we haven't had more Lincolns."

For tourists at the other end of the country, the Empire State Building (completed in time to serve as a backdrop for the movie hit *King Kong*) and Rockefeller Center put wealth and power on display. The labor-oriented mural by famed Mexican artist Diego Rivera, commissioned and completed for Rockefeller Center, was judged by the Rockefeller family too sympathetic to the radical vision of society, depicting worker against capitalist, and was effaced from the walls. A similar mural by Rivera for the Detroit Institute of the Arts, emphasizing the factory process and the dignity of labor somewhat more, survived thanks to the artistic appreciation of family member Edsel Ford.

THE FACE OF AMERICAN RACISM: J. EDGAR HOOVER

The idealistic goals of racial equality celebrated in some parts of the Roosevelt Administration were not widely held in the United States of the 1930s, even outside the South. In various states including California, laws against interracial marriages were still in effect along with rigid if not legally formal, segregation of most local public facilities and housing. The President himself might, however, have greatly mitigated the legal and extra-legal enforcement of racist standards through one simple measure: the replacement of J. Edgar Hoover as Director of the Federal Bureau of Investigation. The failure to do so significantly slowed progress toward racial equality.

Bits Hayden

Hoover had risen to influence first as the "red hunter" of the late 1910s and early 1920s, combating a supposed threat of subversives by unleashing a suppression of civil liberties unprecedented since the Civil War. He gained new popularity with the pursuit of notorious bank robbers and other criminals of the 1930s. But Hoover, rumored to be a cross-dresser in private while staunchly homophobic in public, also had racial supremacist views not far from those of European fascists.

The Director had a particular, violent hatred for all advocates of racial equality. He considered non-whites to be backward genetically, the very possibility of equality to be a communistic scheme alien to civilization, and the danger of race-mixing a foremost challenge to the rules of society. In later years, he would issue the command to his field offices, "Get the Burrhead!" (that is, Dr. Martin Luther King, Jr.). But many of his smaller political conspiracies remain unknown or underappreciated. In fact, they set the standard for U.S. government spying upon its own citizens, a standard applied heavily in the Vietnam era and still very much in effect in the twenty-first century.

Roosevelt, for his own reasons, stayed clear of removing or even criticizing Hoover, who meanwhile used his new-found popularity to increase his influence, infiltrate political organizations and unions with spies, and issue reports (or quiet threats of the blackmail variety) on those who he saw as standing in the way of his prestige and power.

Within the Administration, meanwhile, Eleanor Roosevelt pressed the race issue with her White House invitations, a pressure redoubled after she failed to get black families admitted to the New Deal-created town of Arthurdale, West Virginia, in 1935. Leaders of the NAACP and the historical black colleges attended a meeting at her invitation, and the discussion went on until midnight, when the President was wheeled in to join them.

"BUT, DARLING, WE CAN'T DEPORT *ALL* OF THEM!"

A. Redfield

During the years ahead, Eleanor quietly urged New Deal administrations to spend equal amount of money for education and welfare for whites and blacks in the South, something previously unimaginable, and largely ignored in practice but held up as an ideal. She unsuccessfully urged an anti-lynching bill in Congress, supported by Harold Ickes (who had once been president of the NAACP's Chicago branch), a bill that FDR failed to support because of its political costs to him. She was urged onward by the publicity surrounding the case of the "Scottsboro Boys," unemployed young African-American men falsely accused of raping a young white woman while riding in a box car with her, and sure to be sentenced to death until a public defense campaign led by Communists and W.E.B. Du Bois of the NAACP managed to save their lives if not spare them from prison.

In 1936, Eleanor invited the famed African-American contralto singer, Marian Anderson, to sing at the White House. This was a stunning public symbol of social intimacy, and the press reported the friendliness of FDR along with the President's wife on that memorable evening. It was one of the most surprising symbols of changes taking place at the highest levels of American life.

Chapter 4

New Deal at the High Water Mark

THE REAL (NEW) DEAL

The years between 1935 and 1940 may be considered the grandest days of the New Deal and the most important for American domestic life in the entire twentieth century. The sweeping reforms that constrained the power of otherwise unlimited personal and corporate wealth, while also providing basic relief for the most indigent, were set in place here. Working people, through organized labor and social movements, exerted their maximum popular influence before the mechanisms of war-production and the bureaucratization of labor organizations constrained the promise of further participation and influence. Wartime would bring employment and better material lives to a large part of the population; but these gifts arrived with a price tag that would never grow smaller.

Franklin Roosevelt felt understandably buoyant in the several months after the 1936 election, as the year 1937 approached and dawned. With sweeping Democratic congressional victories, his re-election was a triumph of a kind he was never to enjoy again.

The Inauguration, six weeks earlier than previously—this thanks to the Twentieth Amendment, aimed at getting new presidencies swiftly underway—happened on a miserably rainy Washington day. FDR determined to give his speech outdoors, and his son James held the President's arm. He told the crowd that there had been a people's revolution of sorts in the previous four years, a victory that had "reined in the powers of private autocracy." And yet, tens of millions of Americans were still "denied the greater part of what the very lowest standards of today call the necessity of life. " In a phrase to become famous, he reflected that he could see "a third of a nation ill-housed, ill-clad, ill-nourished." Americans at large, listening on their radios, seem to have shared his sentiments and roared their approval.

But he had trouble close at hand. Roosevelt's key political advisor for many years, Louis Howe, had died the previous April; post-Inauguration, Roosevelt found himself more personally isolated than ever in terms of political strategy. Just now, he would need strategic advice more than he had than any other time in office. He called in reporters for an announcement on February 5, 1937, telling them that the issue of constitutionality had been a central problem and he had information from the Attorney General describing a backload of more than fifty thousand cases, many of them related to the economic collapse. He informed them that within an hour, he would be delivering a message to Congress with a solution.

COURT PACKING

Roosevelt faced many defeats toward the end of the 1930s, but none was more personally painful or decisive in the future of government than his failure to shift the Supreme Court away from property rights and toward human rights. He asked Congress to expand his right to create a new Supreme Court appointment as soon as any Justice reached the age of seventy and failed to resign. He could, by this means, conceivably expand the Court from the current nine to a maximum of fifteen justices. Roosevelt claimed credibly that workload of the Court would be reduced, efficiency gained. Everyone knew, however, that this meant a major political shift in one part of government.

Conservative newspapers and Republican politicians cried foul, insisting that Roosevelt was intent on "packing" the Court with his allies. The natural enemies of the Administration were joined, in an unusually wide protest against this popular president, by other groups and individuals from practically all sides of the political spectrum. Newspaper editorials complained that the division of powers would be eroded if not entirely overthrown. Some well-known progressive figures including reformist Amos Pinchot, Senator Burton K. Wheeler and left-leaning *New Yorker* humorist Dorothy Parker, vented outrage at the over-concentration of personal power. Democratic insiders concluded correctly that it was a bad strategic move for the president, one that he could not win. Roosevelt turned to the Fireside Chat, telling listeners that in a three-horse team pulling for progress, one horse now refused to pull, and that Americans themselves, properly in the driver's seat, deserved unity of effort.

The struggle for public opinion went on from spring into summer, with no improvement in public opinion for the measure. Asked if they would vote for FDR as president again, fewer responded positively. But something remarkable had happened near the end of March. The Supreme Court decided that a Washington state minimum wage law could be allowed—a 5-4 vote that signified one crucial mind, probably that of Justice Owen Roberts, had apparently been changed. The existing Court had got the message: key justices began supporting other New Deal measures, especially Social Security and the National Labor Relations Act. Roosevelt had won the legal war (and settled on a successful compromise that shuffled lower court procedures) but Republicans would go after further New Deal projects with intent to kill. In truth, the President never seemed to be invincible again. This was the signal that conservatives, and not only Republicans, had waited for.

LABOR CONSOLIDATES STRENGTHS

The formation of a Congress of Industrial Organizations(*i.e.*, a distinct labor federation of industrial unions) in 1938 confirmed the division of the labor movement into bitterly competing factions. Conservatives stood almost entirely in the AFL, with FDR-style liberals and out-right radicals in the CIO, although local conditions often trumped these large differences. AFL leaders had initially opposed even minimum wage legislation a few years earlier, believing that only unions of skilled workers were entitled to make such decisions—for their own members. Now they no longer represented the leading influential edge of labor. The sit-down strikes of 1936-1937 marked the high point of industrial democracy, thrusting the New Deal leftward as the earlier city "general strikes" of 1934 had done. Contrary to conservative charges, these strikes, marked by seemingly spontaneous impulses of workers at particular factories to refuse work and also refuse to leave the premises, were not the products of Communist conspiracy. Moving in a wave-like motion from one region to another, engaging factories, stores and other locations (housewives by the hundreds staged their own sit-down strikes for better treatment and less thankless drudgery), the strikes peaked in their significance in Flint, Michigan. There, in two of the largest automobile factories in the world, strikers took over facilities at the end of December, 1936, demanding recognition by management of their union, the United Auto Workers.

Michigan National Guardsmen prepared for what would have been a violent confrontation to recover control of company property, but the Democratic governor of the state, Frank Murphy, successfully achieved peaceful resolution, with quiet support from FDR. The strikers won their case. In working toward victory during weeks of factory occupation, they had also created their own infrastructure of rules and regulations, leisure and education. Many union leaders were hesitant about the radical implications involved in the seizure of private property, even for tactical purposes. But the case for peaceful "direct action" seemed decisive. In future generations, the factory "sit in" would be seen as precedent for the anti-segregationist "sit in," and for the campus "teach in" against the Vietnam War.

The results were spectacular in terms of working and living conditions. Steelworkers unions and auto workers unions alone, by the end of 1937, totaled three quarters of a million members, the CIO at large soon four million. These union members and millions of others achieved something considered impossible only a few years earlier, including a 40-hour week, decent wages, paid vacations and a degree of influence in daily factory activities. For many, it meant family exit from the slums and money set aside for emergencies or children's education. Until wartime pushed many workers into the military and brought in new populations unused to challenging foremen, it also meant a rudimentary "industrial democracy." A factory group might stop work at any time, encouraged by the union leaders or not, to halt abuse of a fellow worker, to protest dangerous working conditions, or some other immediate cause.

John Heliker

"I TOLD you we'd be shunned socially if you signed that agreement with the C.I.O."

Not every battle was won—not by a long shot. Chicago police provided a lesson in non-peaceful direct action in 1937. As the Steel Workers Organizing Committee of South Chicago seemed poised to break through with unionization, Republic Steel management responded by stockpiling grenades, bombs and tear gas. A crowd of union supporters gathered at a neighborhood tavern and formed an impromptu parade to end a social event, but suddenly, Chicago police charged the group on the street. Firing into the crowd, pursuing men, women and children with clubs and tear gas bombs, dragging them into paddy wagons, the police killed ten with gunfire. The momentum of the industrial union movement was suddenly broken, although unionization of some of the most recalcitrant companies would be achieved during wartime and for the sake of war production.

The labor movement, both CIO and AFL, had meanwhile managed, despite failures in the South, in agriculture and in most small businesses, to grow by leaps and bounds. The Supreme Court confirmation of the NLRA in 1937, allowing a union legitimated by a vote of more than fifty percent of workers to become the official bargaining agent, set off a sudden gold rush for membership. It was, of course, also crucial for the Democrats' potential political leverage. Unions were fast becoming the single most important support for Democrats, along with the "solid" but also deeply conservative South.

Equally important, the CIO unions supported the most progressive social programs of the Roosevelt presidency. The fast-growing United Electrical Workers (UE), Farm Equipment (FE), and United Auto Workers alone constituted a mighty force with distinctly radical leaders and many socialistic members. Other unions that had managed to survive hard times, those with large new memberships (the Amalgamated Clothing Workers and United Mine Workers, to name two) and those few building upon triumphs earlier in the decade (the International Longshore and Warehouse Union, on the West Coast, in particular), were heavily in the Roosevelt camp. Even a small CIO union such as the west-coast Marine Cooks and Stewards could offer unusual democratic or inclusive features: it was reputed to the mostly heavily gay (male) labor organization in the world.

Offering conservative, employer-friendly, often racially "lily white" alternatives in many places to CIO unions, those unions staying within the AFL frequently highlighted suspicion or hatred of Roosevelt and his programs. Among leaders of the powerful garment unions, David Dubinsky regarded the consolidation of the CIO as a conspiracy hatched between the White House and the Communist Party. Dubinsky took his union, the International Ladies Garment Workers, back into the AFL, and concocted his own conspiracies to steal members of assorted CIO unions from their elected leaders. His garment district rival, Sidney Hillman of the Amalgamated Clothing Workers, meanwhile became a special favorite of the White House and helped to draft labor legislation. A few years later, Roosevelt would be heard to shout "Clear it with Sidney!" to many requests for details of programs or appointments.

Consolidation of the labor movement also led to its own sets of contradictions, for working people as well as for FDR. The mercurial John L. Lewis, at first promising to support the formation of a national labor party to run against Democrats and Republicans in 1940, changed his mind, supported Roosevelt's opponent, and withdrew his coal miner members from the CIO.

THE "ROOSEVELT RECESSION"

The economic recession opening in August of 1937 prompted the greatest domestic crisis of the Roosevelt presidency. It hardly compared in scale with the 1929 catastrophe, but it was serious: the stock market went sharply down, corporate profits sunk by up to 80 percent, factories closed, rich people again lost pots of money they had invested, and enemies of the New Deal rushed to blame the president and his programs. Even some earlier supporters complained that business was being investigated too much for wrongdoing, in ways that proved demoralizing to them. In fact, Roosevelt had himself partly to blame: he cut federal expenditures as the economy improved through 1936, believing the worst of the Depression to be over. Conservative critics complained of a "Roosevelt Recession," even though the most likely causes could be found in the retrenchment that they had urged. The way back up, these critics continued to insist, was a balanced budget and lower taxes on profits. A "conservative manifesto" issued by Congressmen hostile to the New Deal late in 1937 consolidated their complaints.

Younger New Dealers in particular took the other side of the argument: the problem of the economy was that not enough money and effort were being spent on programs that put people back to work and otherwise lift them to spend and to improve their lives. Contrary to the claims of Roosevelt's critics, these New Dealers were looking not to Karl Marx but to John Maynard Keynes, the British economist

William Gropper

who believed in government intervention and whose classic tome, *The General Theory of Employment, Interest and Money*, had appeared in 1936. The book was too dense for FDR to read himself, but he got the main point. Businessmen needed to be regulated for their own and the public good, in both the short and long run.

Roosevelt's middle path echoed his re-election campaign. He railed against the "economic royalists," those guilty of rigging prices, conspiring to resist competition, and generally acting irresponsibly with their power and resources. He tried to deliver a Congressional message that balanced the budget yet opened up more avenues to growth. As the stock market plunged again, Roosevelt again promised business fair treatment but added that the government would not allow anyone to starve, nor would it "abandon its broad purpose to protect the weak, to give human security, and to seek a wider distribution of our national wealth."

The early months of 1938 looked grim indeed. Local agencies in some cities ran out of food to provide the desperate with something to eat; the city of Chicago shut down its relief agencies entirely. Roosevelt hesitated, then threw himself into action, announcing in a Fireside Chat in April that the government would increase public works by a billion dollars for permanent improvements to construction needed in cities, counties and states; $300 million would go to slum clearance, with other outlays for highway construction and repair, flood control and so on. He argued that the defense of democracy, the faith of people in government, demanded it.

Business interests, powerful in the Democratic party as well as among Republicans, were not about the accept any further expansion of New Deal programs willingly. If Roosevelt supporters in Congress sought to set a minimum wage and to put a limit on working hours, they were said to be violating the very nature of the voluntary contract between workers and employers. FDR managed to get through a limitation on child labor, if only for products sold through interstate commerce. He wanted further progressive taxation, especially on capital gains, but southern conservative Democrats joined with Republicans in successfully resisting. Any possible extensive programs based in the Farm Tenancy Act and Housing Act (also known as the Wagner-Steagall Act), both passed in 1937, were deprived of the funds needed to make a significant impact upon poor rural or urban populations.

AT THE FEET of LINCOLN

FDR DID NOT GO OUT OF HIS WAY TO COMBAT RACIAL DISCRIMINATION, BUT ELEANOR DID.

FRANKLIN, YOU SHOULD NOT ALLOW NEGROES TO BE PAID LESS THAN WHITES IN THE WPA.

BUT I HAVE TO DEAL WITH SOUTHERN DEMOCRATS IN CONGRESS!

THEY'RE MOVING TO THE NORTH, WHERE THEY CAN VOTE.

well, in that case...

BY EXECUTIVE ORDER, HE BANNED DISCRIMINATION IN WPA PROGRAMS.

FRANKLIN, YOU SHOULD CREATE A DIVISION OF NEGRO AFFAIRS IN THE NATIONAL YOUTH ADMINISTRATION.

WHO WOULD DIRECT IT?

MY FRIEND MARY MCLEOD BETHUNE.

DAUGHTER OF FORMER SLAVES, FOUNDER OF SCHOOLS, SHE LED A GROUP OF ROOSEVELT ADVISORS KNOWN AS THE BLACK CABINET.

SHE HAD A WAY OF GETTING WHAT SHE WANTED.

SHE HAD THE FIRST LADY'S EAR, AND SHE URGED AFRICAN AMERICANS TO ABANDON THE PARTY OF LINCOLN.

Sugar?

NOW WE HAVE THE WPA. WHAT HAVE THE REPUBLICANS DONE FOR US SINCE LINCOLN DIED?

BUT ELEANOR'S GREATEST ACHIEVEMENT AGAINST RACISM WAS MORE SYMBOLIC THAN SUBSTANTIVE.

A MAJOR TALENT HAD BEEN NURTURED BY HER SOUTH PHILADELPHIA COMMUNITY.

WE'LL SEND OUR BABY CONTRALTO TO EUROPE

MARIAN ANDERSON WAS A SENSATION IN THE FINEST CONCERT HALLS IN EUROPE.

Enchantè!

SHE WAS THE FIRST AFRICAN AMERICAN EVER TO PERFORM AT THE WHITE HOUSE.

BUT WHEN SHE TRIED TO BOOK THE TOP CONCERT HALL IN WASHINGTON DC, OWNED BY THE DAUGHTERS OF THE AMERICAN REVOLUTION— (D.A.R.)

SORRY, OUR CONTRACT SAYS "WHITE ARTISTS ONLY."

PEOPLE ARE OUTRAGED AT THE DAR, AND I'M A MEMBER. WHAT GOOD WILL COME OF MY RESIGNING QUIETLY?

I'LL WRITE ABOUT IT IN MY NEWSPAPER COLUMN.

I feel obliged to send in to you my resignation. You had an opportunity to lead in a very enlightened way, and it seems to me your organization has failed.

IT WAS THE FIRST PROTEST AGAINST RACISM BY A RESIDENT OF THE WHITE HOUSE.

101

RACE AND THE SOUTH

The Democratic "Solid South" white vote was always crucial to Roosevelt. It was also unshakably committed to racial segregation as a necessary facet of white superiority, either by reasons of civilized "evolution" (whites were centuries ahead) or according to a more crude but widely popular theory, biology (nonwhites were said to be closer to apes). In some regions outside the South, especially small towns in former Union border states, "Nigger read and run" signs could still be seen, proof that nonwhites were not permitted to stay overnight and needed to move on or face considerable risks.

It only became fully clear decades later that the benefits given by the New Deal to white working people actually had the indirect effect of separating the economic opportunities of the races further. In these tough times, millions of white families gained a degree of social stability, unemployment assistance, housing credits and other benefits while minority families, trapped in a worsening poverty, enjoyed few of these. Most labor-movement leaders and members, with the notable exception of Communists and Socialists, shared the prevailing racial views. In the largely non-union south, construction trade union locals sometimes doubled as Ku Klux Klan chapters when night fell. Leaders of the AFL had threatened, in 1935, to withdraw support from the proposed National Labor Relations Act if it included agricultural and domestic workers—i.e., the majority of non-whites in the workforce (and many women as well).

Roosevelt had made many concessions to Southern Democrats along the way, most especially in agricultural subsidies that would allow planters to throw tenants (including large numbers of African-Americans) off the land while collecting benefits. Now he was going after them along with other Democratic conservatives. He made it a point in the winter and spring of 1938 to set out goals for electing progressives.

Roosevelt gave a major address in March, 1938, in Georgia, calling for the end to the "feudal state" in the South that was, he suggested, not much different from the "Fascist system"—strong words indeed. Two months later he sent a telegram to the NAACP wishing it success in advancing the race and advancing American democracy in the process. His war of words, naming the South as the "number one problem" in the nation, continued but dealt mostly with the virtues of the New Deal for southern economic progress. The three liberal candidates who he backed for nomination in Georgia, South Carolina and Maryland all lost to conservative Democrats who railed against African-Americans and against any interference in southern customs by "Yankee politicians" and their "nigger loving" supporters. With these defeats, the vision of black voters leading the way to a democratic (and Democratic) rebirth disappeared. Only Martin Luther King, Jr., and the civil rights movement of the 1950s could bring that day closer, but not for the tens of thousands of families driven from the land and region economically in the meantime.

There were still other major losses in the elections, in the form of radical third parties. The Minnesota Farmer Labor Party, pushing the New Deal forward from the left, had rolled up a decisive victory in 1936 with a governor and a majority of congressional representatives. The future looked bright. Only two years later, a combination of internal divisions and a massive conservative campaign against "Jewish Red Conspirators" destroyed Farmer Labor prospects, setting the stage for a middle of the road Democratic party to take power and wipe out the competition. Likewise, next door: abandoning as hopeless his effort to launch a national third party for peace and accelerated social progress, Wisconsin's Progressive Party governor Phil La Follette warned that the approaching war would pump up the economy and Democrats would abandon the New Deal mood at an early opportunity. Wisconsin Progressives went down to defeat against Democrats in 1938, never to rise again (among its defeated candidates for state office was the father of Russ Feingold, a leading antiwar progressive in the twenty-first century Senate). Likewise, New York State's American Labor Party was fractured in 1940 and never regained its leading role as idealist champion.

Roosevelt did not suffer anything like total defeat. Crucial southern New Dealer Claude Pepper, a strong supporter of racial equality, faced with what seemed a tough, aggressively racist Republican opponent in Florida, easily won re-election. Optimists reflected that the Republican victories in the House and Senate were sometimes by the narrowest of margins. The Democratic Party still held onto majorities, if just barely.

RELIEF AND THE PUBLIC VISION

Relief programs, steadily evolving, offered examples of these issues, because the familiar conservative assumptions about the "undeserving poor" had been abandoned, but no alternative firmly established. The Federal Emergency Relief Agency (FERA), for example, had been divided into two programs in 1935, the Rural Rehabilitation Program (or RRP) for the countryside and towns, and the Emergency Work Relief Program (EWRP) for city residents. The RRP, with less than a quarter million families enrolled, proved to be less important, although it allowed some rural dwellers to stay in their homes while others, long dependent on a single industry now vanished, could move elsewhere. The EWRP, aimed at white-collar workers, essentially replaced the CWA and early FERA, offering less intrusive investigations for eligibility and thereby removing some of the stigma of "taking relief." But while white women were considered too delicate for physical labor, African-American women were sent to work on government projects with picks and shovels until complaints were heard that such paying labor had not been offered first to white women. These projects were soon dropped entirely.

By the end of the decade, 650,000 miles of highways had been built or repaired, along with every part of city streets, culverts, traffic lights, landscaping, drainage ditches, culverts and so on. The approximately 125,000 public buildings created or repaired included 40,000 or so schools but also hospitals, gyms, fire houses, jails and others for government uses. Swimming pools, playgrounds, parks, band shells, tennis and golf facilities and more brought larger publics into recreational activities, and for the historical-minded, markers and monuments went up by the hundreds. Many of the projects including the formal establishment of the Soil Conservation Service in 1935, were "ecological" before the word was coined: not only the trees planted by the millions in CCC activities but flood and erosion control through earthen dams, replanting of native species, and facilitation of better farming methods, with instruction intended, for example, to help farmers avoid catastrophes like "dust bowl" erosion.

The accelerated development of projects in and around the Tennessee Valley Authority (established in 1933) was destined to be one of the most innovative and potentially far-reaching of all New Deal efforts. Before the end of the war just ahead, TVA would become the largest single producer of electrical energy in the country. Experts from the North and West had transplanted themselves, sometimes for short periods and sometimes for the rest of their careers, to direct the electric energy produced into homes, farms and businesses across the region, but also to help residents improve crop yields, to create better conservation habitat for wildlife and for fish in particular. In the process, TVA introduced unionization through its own employment for at least skilled and semi-skilled workers in a region where unions had been fiercely opposed. Its specialists also helped the population to escape the malaria that had infected large parts of the population.

The TVA epitomized a larger vision unrealized. Two Republican presidents before FDR and a raft of congressional conservatives resisted the idea of a government-generated electrical power as a violation of business prerogatives and as a highly dangerous precedent. On the other hand, popular writer and architectural historian Lewis Mumford proposed new cities, with a maximum population of 50,000, built around expansive gardens, and powered by TVA or other counterparts to be created. Attractive market centers reached by footpaths and bridges rather than highways, regional sources of energy, and public transport would not only banish the filth and noise of current cities, but allow for the development of a civic society while encouraging the individual personality and creativity in tune with public needs. Mumford's narrative for a documentary film, *The City*—one of the most popular attractions for the 1939 World Fair in New York—laid out an optimistic, democratic vision of the possible American future.

But the impulse failed. Even the high-level discussion within the Administration of more TVA-type projects was abandoned, and no further enabling legislation was supported let alone proposed by Roosevelt himself. An impulse toward greater environmental regionalism, the possibility of a self-sustaining grassroots democratic structure, was displaced by the familiar focus upon foreign markets as the key solution to problems. That is, the expansion of trade rather than territory now that the geographical limits of the U.S. had been realized, but "expansion" all the same, would bring national salvation.

HEALTH CARE

Perhaps the most lasting accomplishment of the New Deal, alongside Social Security, proved to be the efforts of both the government and the citizenry to improve health care. Working-class women without particular skills found themselves in hospital as aides, unemployed health professionals went to work treating the public, and others served as badly needed health-care helpers in schools, clinics and hospitals. Women constituted more than forty percent of the white-collar occupations.

The Fair Labor Standards Act of 1938 also had a major health benefit. It abolished child labor, still widely used in southern factories until that time, set a national minimum wage at 40 cents per hour and a 40-hour work week. Although not covering rural work or such occupations as housecleaning, leaving out Mexican-American and African-American farm workers and black maids among others, it prompted wage increases for three-quarters of a million, and set the bar higher for future minimum wage increases.

That Franklin and Eleanor Roosevelt became beloved by millions of families for their volunteer effort in public care was something unprecedented. The March of Dimes and the fight against polio were their own triumph. The name, coined by comic performer Eddie Cantor after the movie newsreel "The March of Time," symbolized a national, nonpartisan effort directed at research for the cure of the disease so often striking children, and in these ways different from private foundations set up by rich families as philanthropic gestures. In 1938, Roosevelt made a radio broadcast asking everyone to contribute a dime to the cause, and many Hollywood, radio and Broadway stars joined in the appeal. The Warm Springs Institute where he stayed was already treating children free of charge, and becoming a major center for research of the disease. When Roosevelt died, his face was imprinted upon newly-made dimes, and the "Salk Vaccine" (named after Dr. Jonas Salk) was announced ten years to the day after FDR's death.

NEW DEAL FAILURES

Other major programs grew in size through the course of the 1930s, adding up to a central relationship of government and personal life almost unrecognizable from ten years earlier. Some historians have called these programs the "Third New Deal." In nearly every case, however, the ongoing conflicts between different figures in the Roosevelt Administration, and that pitting the Administration against the business community, sometimes with Congress in the middle, shaped the evolution and outcome. FDR expressed himself ambivalently, Eleanor less ambivalently, and the mystery of Roosevelt's intent remains after all these years, probably nowhere more than in what was called "production-for-use." Should social investments and expanded public programs replace failed private enterprise, or were they only a temporary crutch to be abandoned as business got back on its feet? Supporters of the New Deal, as much as its opponents, were free to believe what they wanted.

For the entire New Deal but especially for the prospects of production-for-use, the 1938 elections proved to be key. Under pressure from conservatives, especially but not only Republicans, the Works Progress Administration was taken over by the Federal Works Agency, and workers were to be directed toward private industry even when the pay was lower than they had earned on WPA. Projects underway or planned for producing goods were now abandoned, as too competitive to private profits. Non-citizens were banned from projects, along with anyone deemed "subversive" (that is, known to belong to any political or fraternal organization considered antithetical to capitalism). The preference for war veterans was now extended to the widows of veterans and wives of veterans who could not find work. "Loyalty" had been inscribed as the model virtue, an idea further underscored by the turn toward war production. Almost five hundred airports were built in anticipation of war use, along with military bases, and recreation and education facilities for military personnel; military clothing and other articles were produced in greater numbers, or reconditioned where possible. Vocational training programs now turned to the military industry, with many white women, but few African-Americans, hired.

Despite all the limitations, some big things had been accomplished. Hardly more than ten percent of WPA money had been spent on wages, yet this amount was vital to working women in the government projects. By 1938, more than fifty percent of women in the WPA projects were doing production-for-use and on those projects, almost 90% of all workers. Sewing products for institutional or hospital needs and household use were the most important, followed by gardening and canning, notably to create food stuffs for poor families. School lunch programs also benefited hugely. But women also repaired damaged books for public institutions, created copies on Braille, renovated worn shoes and made furniture for kindergartens. One of the more controversial projects, building mattresses out of cotton surplus, had been halted earlier and now began again, with more than a million mattresses produced in 1939.

THE APPROACH OF WAR

The clearest warning of war's approach and the contradictory response of ordinary Americans was the Spanish Civil War. Francisco Franco, fascist ally of Hitler and Mussolini, staged an uprising against the elected Spanish government in 1936. German and Italian resources poured in to assist Franco's brutal attacks on civilians (the horrors were dramatized for the world by Pablo Picasso's painting *Guernica*). Communists and an assortment of other radicals raced toward the defense of the Republic, sending volunteer soldiers and medical aid; meanwhile funds were raised through a global publicity campaign. Americans reacted warily, fearing the spread of war, and the Catholic Church avidly supported Franco as defender of the faith against atheists. After years of bloody fighting, Loyalist forces were defeated, and anti-fascist survivors returned to the U.S. and other countries. Fascism had not been beaten back in a major test of strength, and for that reason alone, world war had probably become inevitable. Mussolini's conquest of Ethiopia, the historian African monarchy, had already added to the sense of dread—and the racial dimension of the unfolding horror.

Meanwhile, Franco's intimate allies, Hitler and his Nazi supporters, tightened the screws upon German citizens. In 1938, "Kristallnacht" (named for the breaking of glass) riots of thugs against Jews revealed the state of terror. Communists were arrested along with others deemed racially "inferior" or politically "anti-social," including homosexuals and the first wave of Jews, Roma (Gypsies) and the handicapped. By 1939, the earliest of the soon massive concentration or "Death" camps was opened at Dachau.

Alongside the ongoing drama in Spain and Central Europe, it was the Japanese assault on China in 1937 that shocked Americans in news abroad—and moved the Roosevelt Administration closer to war. In the last weeks of 1937, an American gunboat, the Panay, had been patrolling the Yangtze River, in accordance with treaties allowing virtual colonial control of large parts of Chinese territory. Japanese warplanes attacked the Panay, as they continued their assault upon the Chinese mainland. The ship sunk, three Americans died and eleven others were wounded.

Bits Hayden

President Roosevelt ordered his Secretary of State, Cordell Hull, to begin an investigation, and seek apologies and compensation from the Japanese. The Japanese response was unsatisfying, barely an admission of a mistake. Meanwhile, a leading Republican conservative in Congress observed that "We should have been out of China long ago," a sentiment shared by a wide swath of the American public.

Disappointments at home have historically turned American presidents toward foreign affairs to make their mark upon the times. Roosevelt faced, however, daunting prospects for peace or security. Japan showed no backward steps in its plans to conquer all Asia, and Hitler grew still bolder as he faced wavering opposition among Germany's European neighbors. Leading figures of old wealthy families, more worried about Communism than Nazism, sometimes hinted that they viewed Germany as the likely winner of any future European war and were willing to accept that outcome rather than resist. On the Continent and in Britain, avowedly racist popular movements formed shock troops, sometimes with the quiet cooperation of police and other authorities. Meanwhile, the Neutrality Act of 1935, enacted amid a continuing wave of disillusionment with Woodrow Wilson's deceptive war agenda almost twenty years earlier, was reinforced by Congressional fiat in 1936 and again in 1937. According to the first revision, loans could not be made to belligerents. According to the second, the purchases of American goods, by any side in a war, had to be carried away by non-American ships, and all weapons sales were to be embargoed.

These measures, retrospectively, might possibly have prevented President Wilson from shifting the U.S. into war in 1917, but the world situation had changed greatly since. Roosevelt hoped to sway public opinion while skirting the letter of the law. His sense of urgency grew with the agreement of British prime minister Neville Chamberlain to win "peace for our time" by agreeing to Hitler's demand to occupy Austria and Czechoslovakia. This notorious "Munich Pact" only encouraged Hitler (and assorted European sympathizers) and gave the Soviets good reasons to feel abandoned in the face of the threat of invasion from their West. Roosevelt was sure that the U.S. had not yet prepared itself for war, and was probably relieved to gain time. His rhetoric described "the lives of millions of men, women and children … lost under circumstances of unspeakable horror," but included no threats of intervention or even an American commitment to help the suffering. He added that "The Government of the United States has no political involvements in Europe, and will assume no obligations in the conduct of present negotiations," as flat an evasion as any the President was likely to make. The Soviets, for their part, moved toward the Non-Aggression Pact signed with the Germans in 1939. They, too, needed to borrow time.

Nothing so epitomized the humanitarian crisis as the situation of German Jews desperate to leave an unwelcome homeland. American conservatives and liberals alike, along with leaders of American organized labor, had successfully demanded the immigration-restrictive legislation of 1926 and now it proved difficult if not impossible to make an exception. Roosevelt extended the visas of some fifteen thousand German Jews living in the U.S. for another six months and then another six, while reassuring Congress that these resident aliens would not be allowed citizenship, and that he would not seek a revision of the immigration quota in law. Millions who might have been otherwise spared could not find a safe haven in America.

THE APPROACH OF THE 1940 ELECTION

At this critical juncture, wearied and unwell, Roosevelt approached the prospect of the 1940 election, pondering a third term that no previous two-term president had ever sought. If his son, James, once observed that FDR was a lonely man by choice, the truism advanced with the passage of time: "Of what was inside him, of what really drove him, Father talked with no one."

Behind him, around him, others gave their answers already: they needed him and America at large needed him. He was saved, as the economy itself was saved, by the global crisis leading to world war. The war broke out in Europe in 1939, and the manufacturers of weapons, aircraft, tanks, ships, trucks, blankets, uniforms and other materiel lobbied for the foreign policies that would bring the orders from Europe to American factories—and for a preparation for war that would bring unprecedented defense dollars into the economy. Before the 1940 election, the orders had begun to flow in from all directions. The economy was already the strongest in a war-torn world.

War had indeed spread. German tanks swept across Denmark and Norway, Holland and Belgium, France fell to the invaders, and Britain's ability to hold off devastation by German bombing seemed fragile. Seeing the future dead ahead, isolationists held rallies in many parts of the country against a threatened repeal of the Arms Embargo. They knew, from experience twenty years earlier, that weapons sales and deliveries would almost certainly bring the U.S. into the war. Former president Herbert Hoover suggested permitting the sale of defensive weapons but not offensive weapons. Roosevelt's own experts gave testimony refuting the difference between these two categories, and isolationists, now led by once-famed flying ace Charles "Lindy" Lindbergh, saw their defeat ahead. The financial pages of leading newspapers announced the repeal of the Embargo with joy, and Southern California boomed with a new rhythm, joined by thousands of new residents in new jobs.

The confusion of Communists and Socialists, with widespread support or sympathy among millions of ordinary Americans, added more complexity to a confused public opinion. Prominent Socialists joined the "Keep America Out of War" movement for a time, while Communist newspapers and speakers suddenly turned antiwar. A shock registered throughout European immigrant populations, especially Jewish Americans who had admired Communists for their antifascist determination, their antiracism and leadership of union drives. Everything seemed to be turning upside down.

Roosevelt's presidential campaign was honed with these difficulties in mind. Republican rallies answered with the theme of "No Third Term Day," and the threat of a fourth Roosevelt term in

William Gropper

the background. The war issue, though, was most important for them as well. Republican candidate Wendell Willkie asked, "Are there any international understandings to put America into the war that citizens do not know about?" He pointed to the deceptions and lies that Woodrow Wilson had told as a Congressional vote for U.S. entry into the First World War approached. Roosevelt found himself promising not to send "American boys" into a European war, although he knew better.

The most unique and unexpected factor in the 1940 campaign was doubtless the Democratic candidate for vice-president: Agricultural Secretary Henry Wallace. No previous candidate for that office had so epitomized the hopes for a more cooperative world ahead, or was seen so much as a thorn in the side of corporate America. In 1940, still the Secretary of Agriculture, he struggled to keep the Forest Service from being transferred to the Department of the Interior, notoriously the tool of the "timber interests" that planned to use the nation's trees for their own profits. Roosevelt actually signed an executive order for that transfer, then tore up his own order. Wallace's determined efforts to prepare the U.S. for global war meanwhile found him urging the production of synthetic rubber, believing correctly that the sources of natural rubber, in the Philippines and East Indies, would soon come under Japanese control. Meanwhile, he urged Pan-American economic cooperation, a more consistently friendly and democratic approach toward Latin America than the wavering Good Neighbor policy.

As the Democratic convention neared, Wallace was described by the press as an odd contender, a man who had never smoked nor drank, an Iowan who knew corn science but not inside politics, and who had a mystical interest in the writings of the ancient prophets. Unlike so many other politicians, Republican or Democratic, he also had no hint of financial corruption in his record.

Republican candidate Willkie, originally from Indiana, was a Wall Street lawyer of somewhat liberal bent, in contrast to his own running mate, a conservative isolationist. The race at first promised to be a hot one. At the Democratic convention, Roosevelt was overwhelmingly renominated but had to convince party leaders about his intended running mate. FDR described Wallace to advisor James Farley as "a philosopher. He's got ideas . . . He'll help the people think." No recent vice-president with the exception of Theodore Roosevelt had ever been much of a thinker, and none had aspired to make ordinary Americans think harder about global problems with long-term, peaceful solutions.

Wallace drove home his version of Rooseveltism on the campaign trail, delivering a speech in Spanish (the first time any presidential or vice presidential speech had been delivered that way), rallying workers and farmers with an intimacy that reminded older listeners of political generations gone by. As the race entered its final weeks, Willkie seemed to pull close again, but the intensifying German air attack on Britain spread fears that Hitler would be successful in conquering all of Europe. In the end, the largest number of voters ever (fifty million) went to the polls and Roosevelt won handily, although Willkie won more votes than any Republican ever had before.

Chapter 5

Doctor Win the War

THE WAR AND THE PRESIDENT

The last years of Franklin Roosevelt's presidency seemed, at least from the standpoint of later decades, to have been almost entirely about World War II. At a closer glance into the daily lives of Americans, and at a closer glance into the operation of government, the war effort framed a sweeping change in domestic life. Prosperity returned, not everywhere but widely, through a level of federal, state and local government in the economy and social life unprecedented, even during the Depression. Changes that would shape the future setting of race conflicts for and against equality for nonwhites grew with the massive migration of formerly rural populations from the South to northern cities, and from Mexico to the Southwest. The activist backbone of FDR's election campaigns, organized labor, underwent fundamental change, bringing both institutional success and seemingly irreversible bureaucratization.

Through all of this and through increasing illness, Roosevelt himself maintained his aplomb. No one, not even those close to him, knew exactly what he had in mind for his next move, nor did many beyond his inner circle guess how his health deteriorated. Roosevelt did not live to complete the victory in the Pacific, nor did his negotiations among the Allies bring anything resembling a lasting world peace. The America that emerged actually seemed hell-bent on another global conflict with potentially more devastating results. Yet the wartime of Roosevelt was a time of great hope and a final moment of a shared sense of American destiny that would disappear too soon when the Axis was defeated.

Bits Hayden

THE NEW GULLIVER
Fred Ellis

In the weeks after the Japanese invasion of Pearl Harbor on December 7, 1941, the mood and tempo of the nation changed suddenly. A sense of national unity emerged rapidly, without the flagrant violations of civil liberties, the shutdown of the antiwar press, the mass arrests and violence against dissenters, that had marked the war mobilization of 1917. But behind the scenes, things were not so simple.

THE WAR AND THE SOVIETS

Events in June, 1941, added an entirely new dimension to the global crisis months before the attack on Pearl Harbor. Hitler's armies invaded the Soviet Union, ending the eighteen-month "non-aggression pact" between the two world powers. Overnight, loyal Communists throughout the world returned to the anti-fascist agenda that had been their strongest source of popular appeal from the middle 1930s to 1939. Within months, they began to re-organize as the heart of a Resistance movement gathering eventually behind the lines across occupied Europe. Communists in Asia, especially, combined their longtime aspiration for independence from colonialism with an anti-fascist urgency, twin goals that unnerved British officials and left American conservatives, and more than a few liberals and State Department officials, increasingly wary of the war's outcome in the resource-rich Third World.

At first, the direction of the war had been strongly in Germany's favor, and in Japan's favor in Asia, at least until the final months of 1942. By conquering so much of Europe, Hitler had gained access to the natural resources, factories and farms of huge regions, including the oil fields of the Caucasus in the USSR. Living standards of German citizens actually continued to rise, while slave labor awaited ever larger numbers of Eastern Europeans. The brunt of German's Eastern Front attack fell upon the Soviet Union, slaughtering civilians and initially crushing "Red Army" resistance. Meanwhile, the Japanese successfully took control of the Philippines and would have swept much of the Pacific but for the successful U.S. sea battles in 1942 in the Coral Sea and at Midway.

But 1942 also held the crucial turning point of the war. Like Napoleon's army more than a century earlier, the Germans found themselves in the middle of the Russian winter, their supply lines overextended. Soviets in the hundreds of thousands answered the call to resist. For the first time in this war, German troops lost confidence. Soon, the Soviet Red Army massed in defense at Stalingrad (now Volgograd), a key industrial city on the Volga River. Here, the German Army experienced the single most decisive defeat anywhere on the globe. In the fight for Stalingrad, the USSR lost more soldiers than the U.S. lost in the entire war.

Seeking to recover by mechanical power, the Germans launched a tank battle in Kursk in 1943, using vast quantities of what they had brought with them, and the Soviets met in similar force. This was the biggest tank battle in human history (and still remains so), six thousand tanks and two million troops altogether. A defeated German army could now only hope to slow the counter-advance of the Red Army, and morale fell among fascist supporters in many parts of the world. Hitler's long-term aim, to wipe out Slavic populations entirely and replace them with "Aryans," had now become unrealizable.

This counter-attack was crucial for many intertwined reasons. After 1920, "Americanism" had been defined by its opposition to "Communism." No one could say exactly what either term meant, but the leading role of big business, along with freedom of speech and religion, defined major differences in worldview and practices. During 1939-41, when Communists joined the swelling peace movement in order to buy time for Soviet regroupment, conservatives leaped at the chance to decry them as subversives, spies, and Jews. In Los Angeles, witnesses at hearings of the House Committee on Un-American Activities blasted Hollywood as run by disloyal Jewish-Americans disguising themselves by taking on Gentile names and poisoning the minds of the young. Then things whirled around, almost exactly in the other direction. Communists and those sympathetic were soon again in the forefront of anti-fascist idealism, especially in the film industry, but also in many immigrant neighborhoods, especially Greek, Slavic, Hungarian, Armenian and Jewish.

Hollywood became the liberal showplace in many ways. Movies reigned as the supreme cultural contribution of contemporary American society (along with jazz music), seen by larger audiences than ever before—actually climaxing in 1946 before retreating to a steadily lesser role in media. And many popular movies made clear and compelling a vision of democracy and its enemies. Humphrey Bogart in *Casablanca* was the ultimate hero, an anti-fascist veteran of the Spanish Civil War grown cynical but who, at movie's end, gives up his lover (Ingrid Bergman) in order to aid a man seeking to continue his underground campaign against the Nazis.

Swashbuckling hits showed American soldiers, sailors, pilots and Marines in all manner of adventure and self-sacrifice for fellow soldiers and the larger cause. In movies set on the home front, democracy advanced even though comedy, with better roles for women (Katharine Hepburn in the *Woman of the Year* was stunning), for working people, and for "ethnics," though rarely African-Americans (*Stormy Weather* marked the first big budget musical with an all-black cast, however). Liberal Hollywood's Communist writers delivered some of the biggest hits and earned some of the biggest salaries—for writers, that is—in the process. Together with left-leaning actors from the Three Stooges and Lucille Ball to Ronald Reagan (in a few years, he would become an FBI informer and move far rightward), they also raised huge amounts of money for the war effort.

William Gropper

RACE AND THE WAR

During the 1930s, the "Jim Crow" system of racial segregation had remained virtually untouched despite Eleanor's urgency to make democracy real for all Americans. She arranged for Franklin to discuss one very heated issue—the need for specific anti-lynching legislation—with Walter White, head of the NAACP. The President demurred. But real progress was realized through legal strategies and political threats.

Roosevelt had launched another kind of initiative years earlier. Lawyers at the Civil Rights Section (CRS) of the Justice Department, formed in 1939 at the president's request, convinced the Supreme Court in 1941 to weaken the legal basis of the all-white voting primary. Three years later, the justices ruled that the racially discriminatory primary no longer had any legal basis. By way of contrast, Congressional majorities sought to strike a blow at the "poll tax" in 1942 through the Soldier Voting Act (that is, across race lines), only to see Southern senators filibuster the measure to death. Meanwhile, CRS moved ahead with efforts to halt the lynching of African-Americans. Federal attorneys gained only mild legal punishment of individuals among murderous white crowds, but placed future potential murderers on warning. Deeply embarrassed by the international news coverage of American outrages, the CRS also pressed further on race-based police brutality, establishing precedents for later legal action.

A handful of African-American leaders pressed harder for progress. In 1940, A. Philip Randolph, head of the Sleeping Car Porters union, invited Eleanor Roosevelt to attend their annual convention, held in Boston, shrewdly using the opportunity to call for equal treatment in various walks of life. Mrs. Roosevelt accepted the invitation and invited Randolph and Walter White to the White House. The President listened politely as they offered a petition asking the government to ban segregation in both the Armed Forces and in defense production work. Then the President himself bowed to the usual Southern pressures.

For Randolph, this was a double-cross, demanding action. He announced a forthcoming national march on the nation's capitol for July 1, 1940. FDR foresaw a movement of thousands of African-Americans facing the white and deeply racist police force of the city, a potential catastrophe. Eleanor tried, without success, to talk Randolph and White out of the march, but they refused outright until the President agreed to let the two black leaders help draft an executive order. A week before the march was to take place, Roosevelt issued Order 8802, one establishing a Committee on Fair Employment Practice (FEPC): "I do reaffirm the policy of the United States that there shall be no discrimination in the employment of workers in defense industries or government because of race creed, color, or national origin." The march was cancelled—although Roosevelt promised nothing about the integration of the Armed Forces, which remained tightly segregated with non-whites in subordinate positions and often badly treated, for the duration of the conflict.

Race standards also proved difficult to enforce. White workers and union leaders often would not accept their new coworkers. Labor's radicals, in the burgeoning industrial unions, set a high standard, often precipitating counter-responses and the formation of avowedly conservative "ABC" ("Anyone but Communists") union factions within the United Auto Workers, Electrical Workers and elsewhere. Labor conservatives quickly became allied with the Association of Catholic Trade Unionists (ACTU), funded by the Church and working closely with the FBI. Radicals and progressives had an especially hard time in Detroit, where in June, 1943, fears of housing integration and lower home values sparked a white riot, with twenty-five African-Americans and nine whites dead before it was over. Police and National Guardsmen tamed the crowds, but showed no sympathy for nonwhites. In Los Angeles, servicemen on leave attacked Mexican-American youngsters wearing "Zoot Suits," beating the youths and ripping off their clothes—another example, for many, that racist attitudes at home had to be combated along with the fascism abroad. Political activists called their campaign "VVV," victory over Germans, Japanese, and America's home-bred racists.

THE NEW DEAL COMPLETED?

Roosevelt, presenting himself as "Doctor-Win-the-War" in the weeks after Pearl Harbor, offered up a series of domestic programs humbler in scale but in some ways resembling an extension of "Doctor New Deal." The economy, in a slump for more than a decade, had already begun to stumble forward, then race ahead. Suddenly, employers were looking for workers, and geographic mobility reached an all-time high. Minorities and women now entered the workforce at an unprecedented rate. War, some cynics concluded, was the one New Deal economic program that really worked.

No election until 1944 depended more upon labor than that of 1942, when the CIO launched the first Political Action Committee (PAC), a term later most associated with business organizations' gifts to candidates of both parties. CIO-PAC mobilized tens of thousands of union volunteers and hundreds of thousands of dollars from union workers' pockets for FDR's congressional supporters. The 1942 midterm elections nevertheless brought a loss of seats in the Senate and the House, Democrats retaining majorities by a narrow margin. The closure of some major New Deal programs, like the Works Progress Administration with its arts and theatrical programs, was now inevitable and the President did not resist. He had his eyes upon other goals.

But did he still have his New Deal grassroots constituency on his side? Advocates of working people and the poor celebrated the passage of a wartime tax on the rich to a peak of 88% of some incomes, although the powerful still had ways to get around paying their fair share. Meanwhile, profits went through the roof, and prices for food, clothing, and other necessities rose sharply. The rise in employment gave workers more options to strike for better pay and improved conditions, and strike they did, despite pledges of union leaders not to strike in wartime.

William Gropper

John L. Lewis's coalminers went on strike in 1943, over the opposition of other union leaders as well as public pressures, and they won substantial pay increases. The Roosevelt Administration, recognizing

122

the necessity of labor's cooperation in the war effort, encouraged union membership, even against the determination of many conservative corporate leaders to resist at all cost. Major holdouts like the Ford Corporation gave in and union membership rose rapidly from nine to fifteen million members, divided between the two federations. Labor leaders of the CIO and AFL had set out to regularize production in 1942, as the Combined Labor Board and the National War Labor Board met regularly, the NWLB with Roosevelt himself, to remove any obstacles and increase efficiency. In this extended emergency moment, a new labor conservative, George Meany, entered the scene as the leader of a reviving AFL. Rising up in the construction trades where "whites only" rules carried on traditions of giving jobs to sons and nephews of those at work, Meany clawed his way to power, promising to end strikes and establish labor's respectability once and for all. In 1944, he announced his opposition to Roosevelt's re-election. Nevertheless, organized labor in America would never be so influential again.

THE ARSENAL OF DEMOCRACY

The Arsenal of Democracy was world-historic, giving rise to a raft of new agencies with a power unprecedented in the American economy. The Supply Priorities and Locations Board (SPAB), for instance, governed scarce materials and resources considered vital to the war effort, going so far as to end production of some crucial products (such as automobiles) for the war's duration or otherwise limiting amounts produced. The Office of Price Administration (OPA) assisted in this work by making some things beyond the purchasing power of ordinary people. The War Manpower Commission and the National War Labor Board took over the mobilization of the workforce and mediation with a labor movement growingly influential and necessary for expanded, efficient production. Overall, the Office of War Mobilization coordinated the work of thousands of officials in these agencies, and this was only the beginning of what might have been called a Super New Deal—if it were not limited to wartime.

The consequent control of communications, the flow of ideas, would have been condemned by conservatives and suspected by liberals under any other circumstances. As it was, the Office of War Information "sold" the war to the public through radio, films, magazines and newspapers, and also developed propaganda used behind enemy lines. The corporate-owned daily press and radio had, of course, been traditionally pro-business and largely conservative, but somewhat unfocused, less thorough in their anchoring of information to a single viewpoint. The Roosevelt Administration meanwhile created semisecret agencies as the Office of Scientific Research and Development, coordinating military research, and the Office of Strategic Services, forerunner of the CIA, an intelligence operation with secrets kept even from Congress.

The advantages of the U.S. increasing production faster than anywhere else on earth were obvious to enemies and friends alike. Enormous natural and human resources, plenty of land, no bombings, no invasions, and a Congress now willing to spend seemingly unlimited funds made all the difference. Some of the most amazing developments and some of the most permanent were largely regional in nature. The farm population dropped almost twenty percent during the War and never returned to its past importance as a symbolic center of middle American life. The small farmer was replaced in many areas by companies working large sections of land with heavy machinery, pesticides and chemical fertilizers previously unknown but useful for rapidly increasing production. Some 200,000 Mexican workers came to the U.S. on the "bracero" program to pick crops and do railroad work at low wages. In the Southwest and West, areas flooded with military dollars, new cities sprung up and towns turned into zones of manufacture and military bases. Big business also grew suddenly, often at the expense of small-scale manufacturing, although for many small operators, especially commercial trades like corner stores, money was coming in at last.

Not everyone benefited equally, a development less troubling at the time than it would become later. Most troubling, however, was the internment of more than 120,000 Japanese Americans on the premise that they might become disloyal, a notion not applied to German or Italian nationals. Most received only a week's notice to close up their homes and businesses, largely but not entirely on the West Coast. As they suspected, they would never be allowed to return to what they had built or created through savings: others, usually prominent local citizens, would take and keep them. The relocation camps, scattered through remote desert areas, were crowded, with inadequate medical provisions, and poor supplies of food and warm clothing. Roosevelt, who signed the executive order in 1942 ordering the internment, seemed to have made a catastrophic error—or given in to the popular mixture of racial superstition and local greed. Only in 1988, after most of the victims had died, did the U.S. Congress offer an apology and minimal reparations for harm done.

FDR's way of operating politically would always be shrouded in mystery, in foreign policy as well as domestic. But as the tide of war turned against the Axis powers, his postwar aims became steadily more clear. He devoted himself to the idea of continuing cooperation with the wartime alliance, especially with the British and Soviets. He thought of the U.S. as first among equals, poised to retain and expand a sort of global balance of powers. He insisted that U.S. troops would not long remain in Europe after the war's end, and he gradually warmed to the idea of something like the old League of Nations, something that became the United Nations, founded months after his death.

FDR, CHURCHILL, STALIN

Looking to war and beyond, FDR abjured the bellicose tone and racial expressions of cousin Theodore, offering democratic promises in their place. He had less to conceal about the U.S. entry into war and behavior than his other distinct predecessor, Woodrow Wilson. The most important difference was, however, the issue of colonies: Teddy Roosevelt had believed in centuries of colonization ahead, Wilson in the independence of these areas of Asia, Africa and elsewhere sometime in the distant future but he accorded captive peoples no "right" to independence. Roosevelt moved close to the idea of self-government for all the world's peoples.

This commitment became all the more crucial as the Allies pressed the counteroffensive against Fascism. In 1942, U.S. forces landed in North Africa, and in 1943, U.S. and British forces invaded the southern tip of Italy, fighting their way northward, unseating the Fascist government but barely recognizing the Italian Communists who led the Resistance. In Asia, the Indian subcontinent and the Pacific, nationalists set out to push back the Japanese, while American "island hopping" began across the Pacific, troops taking one island at a time.

Japanese sea power was to be crushed in the battles of Leyte Gulf and the Philippine Sea in 1944. The Philippines remained a site of tough fighting, with Filipino guerrillas assisted by Americans.

It often seemed in the late months of 1944 and early 1945 that Roosevelt's main critic on the global stage was not Stalin but Churchill, an undaunted imperialist as well as a moody alcoholic and megalomaniac. At the Teheran Conference of November, 1943, Roosevelt made fun of Churchill's personality faults and bad habits, to the great amusement of Stalin. Harry Hopkins, Roosevelt's right hand man, shared the view that Stalin would be flexible if handled right—and Churchill might not be flexible at all.

In Operation Overlord, Americans and their Allies landed on the coast of Normandy, France, in early June, 1944. After great losses, a million soldiers and thousands of vehicles came ashore, breaking through German lines. Ahead lay the Battle of the Bulge, a German counter-attack that could not succeed but brought vast battle deaths on all sides.

Parts of the colonial world were by now on the move, and those who supported the old colonial arrangements or corrupt leaders propped up by Western leaders faced increasingly rough going. Often, New Deal diplomats quietly sympathized with the revolutionaries. Most of all, this was true for China, run by the extraordinarily corrupt Jiang Jieshi who had virtually abandoned the effort to rally his people to fight off the Japanese and now faced a Communist-led army that seasoned American diplomats regarded as the next and best government that China was likely to get. But to accept the victory of Chinese Reds openly would be politically impossible: powerful Americans with commercial aspirations for China, and those with close ties to Christian missionaries there, would not accept Communist leadership as legitimate.

Roosevelt compounded the problem and helped lay the basis for future misuse of power by allying or establishing a careful détente with some of the most resolute fascists and their supporters. Mass murderer Francisco Franco had wisely adopted formal neutrality in the War. Meanwhile, Roosevelt's State Department arranged what insiders would call the "Vichy Gamble," a secret agreement with the Hitler-appointed government of France, resisting neither the discrimination against French Jews, the theft of French Jewish property nor the deportation of French Jews to concentration death camps. Across Europe, where old semi-aristocratic classes had first bowed to German invaders but now looked for ways to bail out, American diplomats wavered between cooperation with the armed Resistance and seeking exiled conservatives and liberals who would be placed into power after the war, promising to protect private property and American investments.

Some American corporate leaders had themselves been hedging bets all along. As with the German division of General Electric and several other major corporations, U.S. investors in I.G. Farben continued to earn profits during the war, through an arrangement with German government cooperation.

CURFEW HOUR IN BERLIN   Jacob Burck

YALTA

Yalta, a Soviet port on the Black Sea, had been chosen as location of a secret meeting of Stalin, Churchill and Roosevelt, along with their respective staffs. To those who had not seen the president in years, he looked terrible, despite his cheerful manner. Meeting in a old Czarist palace above the sea, diplomats quickly recognized the obvious: the three leaders had very different objectives, perhaps more so as the end of the war came almost into sight. Roosevelt wanted to create a

United Nations but also to see the Soviet Union come into the war against Japan just as soon as possible after the Germans were defeated. Churchill wanted to keep the British Empire intact and if possible, secure British control over a defeated Europe. Stalin wanted absolute security for the Soviets against another attack from its western borders.

Poland's future became a central issue, notwithstanding the occupation of the country by Soviets pushing back the Germans. Would it ever again be the route for invasion that it had been for Napoleon and Hitler alike? Roosevelt accepted Soviet control, with a minimum of concessions, in return for an agreement that the USSR would declare war on Japan within three months after Germany's surrender.

Returning home, Roosevelt addressed a joint session of Congress on March1, 1945, and for the first time, showed in public that he had a disability. No previous president had done so but he had little choice: he was brought to the front in a wheelchair and spoke seated in a soft chair rather than standing. Long in the dark about Roosevelt's condition, the public now recognized something hidden all along.

SHADOWS OF THE COLD WAR

The structural underpinnings of the emerging Cold War lay in the fate of a devastated Europe and beyond: what system would inhabitants choose or have chosen for them in the prospect of reconstruction? The idea of a peaceful, global 'condominium' ruled mainly by the U.S. and the USSR with other nations participating or compliant, seemed to have been made institutional in the plans for United Nations, founded in 1945. Then things fell apart or were caused to fall apart in ways unforeseen by FDR, with staggering consequences for the accomplishments of the New Deal. How could allies turn into adversaries so quickly, and had the fault been Roosevelt's own naivete toward the Soviets or some flaw in his global vision?

Roosevelt had definitely not reconciled in his own mind, let alone settled it with world leaders, the conflicting aspirations of the U.S. and the USSR. For a century, Americans had ruled Latin America, with all but the last vestiges of European competition fading away during the war and long-term U.S. leases on British bases in the Caribbean extending Americanization in the region. The threat of

Japan and Germany had confirmed the belief of powerful corporate and government figures that the U.S. must dominate the Pacific as well as the Western Hemisphere with a global network of military bases, across Western and Central Europe, the oil-rich Middle East, even East Asia.

The U.S., source of a staggering fifty percent of the world's goods and services by 1944, was in a commanding economic position if markets were opened to "free trade," or rather, international trade upon conditions that the U.S. considered favorable to itself. At Bretton Woods, New Hampshire, late in 1944, world delegates seemed to endorse these U.S.-friendly positions and related commercial rules in the creation of new U.S.-dominated world bodies, the World Bank and the International Monetary Fund.

Against this vision of an "American Century" stood a great deal of history, especially but not limited to Russian history. No nation, not even England at its nineteenth-century apex, had ever dominated such large sections of the planet effectively. And worse: across the colonized world, elites had been shaken and the old rules had been changed by war, most especially the racial assumptions of white over nonwhite. Soviet losses included twenty million dead—one person in almost every extended family—and the destruction of two thousand cities and towns, seventy thousand villages and hamlets, and more than 30,000 factories. Little agriculture remained, as crops were ruined along with tens of millions of hogs, cattle, goats, sheep and horses, all slaughtered.

Contrasting national aspirations compounded ideological differences that had seemed to be lessening, but could now grow greater again at any time. Both Soviet leaders and ordinary Communists around the world—many of them in positions of greatly heightened importance in 1944, thanks to the war effort—believed capitalism outside the U.S. to be largely exhausted. Whatever they now imagined for the postwar future in various nations (in the U.S., something close to an extended New Deal, with business interests gradually eliminated and racial equality realized), they would not easily accept the return of old-style capitalism or the global hegemony of the Americans, especially not when Wall Street seemed to call the shots.

HENRY WALLACE, SOUL OF THE NEW DEAL

Vice-President Henry Wallace, at the head of the new Economic Defense Board (EDB, later to be renamed the Board of Economic Welfare, BEW) in July, 1941, seemed to bring the mobilization of the country to a new level. FDR additionally appointed Wallace head of the Supply Priorities and Allocations Board a month later. Now he was, by any standard, the most powerful vice-president in the history of the country, the second most powerful figure in Washington, as no previous vice-president had ever been.

He set to work determined, among other things, to prepare Americans for war by increasing agricultural production and ensuring an adequate diet. This was a far cry from the industrial and military view that money for the manufacture of war materiel was the most important (and, of course, highly profitable) project. Wallace also set out to arm the nation morally. He proposed—and Roosevelt enthusiastically agreed—to have Wallace give one major public address per month. He had a great subject, "The Common Man," and his vision extended beyond the war, to social reconstruction. He also added more enemies with each passing month.

The nation was "writing the postwar world as we go along," he explained, and victory would give the U.S. a second chance to do right what was done wrong in 1919. Now the nation could help create a world "where security, stability, efficiency and abundance would prevail." In another radio address, he announced that "Everywhere the common people are on the march." The publisher of *Time* magazine, Henry Luce, had written only a few months earlier that victory would mean the "American Century," a century of unparalleled and perhaps unchallenged U.S. power and influence. Wallace had something different in mind, for in the postwar world there "must be neither military nor economic imperialism" with the powerful dominating and exploiting the weak new nations soon emerging. Colonialism, international cartels, racism and racist culture were, Wallace insisted, finished forever.

Hundreds of thousands of printed copies of this speech went out. Conservatives and southern racists objected, as did the *Wall Street Journal* and even the *New York Times*. Wallace was promising too much. The Catholic Church objected as well. For the time being, Wallace was safe, protected by Roosevelt, who privately agreed that it was essential for the U.S. and the Soviet Union to understand each other better, as the two great nations of the postwar world.

Troubling indications of a different kind of vision, and the prospect of a different kind of world, were rapidly coming into view. Wallace sought a demilitarized postwar Germany, thus removing the threat from Soviet borders. He warned in a speech in March, 1943, that World War III was certain "in case we double-cross Russia" and if the U.S. failed to provide full employment at home.

Perhaps the crucial moment arrived at the last FDR press conference of 1943. *Time* magazine gleefully announced that the New Deal was dead at last. Speaking on Jan. 22, 1944, Wallace offered a different interpretation, saying, "The New Deal is as old as the wants of man ...The New Deal is Abraham Lincoln preaching freedom for the oppressed. The New Deal is Franklin D. Roosevelt." The crowd of Democratic politicians attending the dinner reportedly glowered at him.

His critics, Democrats and Republicans alike, called him a "dreamer" and "mystic" who lacked realism, but FDR called him "Old Man Common Sense" who knew far more about science than his enemies. Wallace traveled to Asia, surveying the economic potential of Russia's Far East, as FDR was signing the G.I. Bill of Rights, the most important measure of productive state assistance since the enactment of Social Security. Wallace traveled on to China, where he failed to get a firm view of the collapse of the government and the fighting against Japanese invaders by forces led increasingly by Communist Mao Zedong.

Wallace seemed not to notice Stalin's use of Siberia as vast political prison camp, nor to grasp the complexities of the Chinese situation. These failures, and Wallace's personal quarrels with other administrators of wartime agencies, helped encourage his enemies within the Democratic Party to campaign against his renomination as vice-president. British officials meanwhile raged at Wallace for proclaiming the end of colonial legitimacy, and influential American opinion leaders, including Walter Lippman, described Wallace as too idealistic to be president in case the ailing president died. Roosevelt, in private meetings, offered no defense of him, while political bosses discussed various alternatives, including the uncontroversial senator from Missouri, Harry Truman.

Wallace remained very popular among ordinary Democrats, rating highest in Gallup polls for favorite vice-presidents, and movie audiences cheered his appearance in newsreels capturing his visit to Asia. He had tapped the American love of the underdog as much as he failed to woo the business class and the political professionals.

HARRY TRUMAN AND THE PARTY BOSSES

At a crucial moment at the Democratic convention in Chicago, August, 1944, the crowd chanted *We Want Wallace!* Observer Studs Terkel later recalled bigger crowds just outside the hall were even more enthusiastic. But at the crucial moment, as Florida senator Claude Pepper strode from the floor toward the podium to nominate Wallace as vice-president, two heavyweight figures dragged him away by the arms. The chairman meanwhile banged the gavel and successfully adjourned the session. Through the night, party bosses set out to secure Truman's nomination and the next day, Chicago police strictly limited entry to the hall. A quick vote was arranged to prevent Wallace's forces from reorganizing, and Truman won the nomination on the third ballot. It was, in a symbolic sense and more, the real end of the New Deal.

Roosevelt never commented on his reasons, but the need for Democratic Party unity was the leading cause. Roosevelt had promised Wallace privately that he would turn in a further liberal direction after the election, and give him the job of Commerce Secretary, presuming the ticket won. They did win overwhelmingly, with strong support from liberals, and with an unprecedented turnout of CIO-PAC supporters raising money and voters. As the Senate wrangled over his appointment, Wallace wrote an extended pamphlet, *Sixty Million Jobs*, in effect the blueprint for a full-employment economy.

Meanwhile, Roosevelt was becoming physically weaker by the day. Even as Allied troops in Europe routed the Germans and the end of the Nazi threat drew near, FDR suffered a massive cerebral hemorrhage and died on April 12, 1945. He was just sixty-three. Roosevelt and his advisors had kept the extent of his deteriorating health a secret.

There was another secret of personal importance. In his final days at Warm Springs, his companion was Lucy Mercer, lover from his early married years. She had been forced away from him and married prominently, later widowed. After Missy LeHand died of a stroke in 1944, he sought out this old flame. Mercer quickly left the scene after FDR's death, yielding to Eleanor and Grace Tully, his "proper" companions.

The funeral train carried him from Georgia to his family home in upstate New York. The days after his death produced an outpouring of national grief unseen in intensity again for any president, even after President John F. Kennedy's assassination fifteen years later. Shortly after Roosevelt's passing, a radio cantata, "The Lonesome Train," about the travel of the train with Lincoln's body to Washington, was replayed on CBS, as directed by famed radio writer-producer Norman Corwin. It had been prepared originally to rouse wartime patriotism by recalling the revered Civil War-era president. Now the cantata fit the national feeling of grief perfectly. Only a few years later, the scriptwriter (a former folksinger with Pete Seeger's Almanac Singers) and director Corwin all found themselves officially or unofficially blacklisted for "subversive" activities or suspicious connections.

The mood changed rapidly in many other small ways as well. Harry Truman's wife Bess and their daughter Margaret were reportedly outraged by Eleanor Roosevelt's lifestyle and her indifference to the physical conditions of the White House. They initiated an extensive refurbishing to restore to the home a grandeur proper for the most powerful family in the world.

There were also changes in American cultural life at large, some coming to the fore around the death of Roosevelt. The movie genre known as "film noir," marked by a dark view of the world seen as a place ready to crush the ideals of any courageous loner, was apparent already in *The Maltese Falcon* (adapted from the novel by Dashiell Hammett) and *Murder, My Sweet* (adapted from another detective novel, by Raymond Chandler), leading to dozens of artistically brilliant films in the later 1940s with similarly pessimistic visions. The grim, existential philosophy of the Cold War-era was steadily emerging, a dog-eat-dog individualism replacing the Depression and wartime sense of national sharing.

Last Days in Warm Springs

MARCH 1945

EXHAUSTED AFTER TALKS AT YALTA WITH CHURCHILL AND STALIN, FDR WENT TO HIS THERAPEUTIC RETREAT IN THE HILLS OF GEORGIA.

THE NEW DEAL'S WORK RELIEF PROGRAMS HAD BEEN ELIMINATED IN THE BOOMING WAR ECONOMY.

STATION

I'VE BEEN COMING HERE SINCE 1924 FOR THE HEALING WATERS.

I BUILT THE PLACE UP TO A MODEL TREATMENT CENTER FOR PEOPLE WITH POLIO.

MY PERSONAL COTTAGE IS KNOWN AS "THE LITTLE WHITE HOUSE."

FROM HERE, WE LAUNCHED THE NATIONAL FOUNDATION FOR INFANTILE PARALYSIS AND THE MARCH OF DIMES.

ON APRIL 12th, FDR SAT FOR A PORTRAIT THAT LUCY HAD COMMISSIONED.

THE PORTRAIT WAS NEVER FINISHED.

I HAVE A TERRIFIC HEADACHE.

THE PRESIDENT SLUMPED OVER.

HE DIED OF A CEREBRAL HEMORRHAGE.

ELEANOR RETURNED A WATERCOLOR SKETCH TO LUCY.

I had NO idea they were still in touch!

WITHIN THE MONTH THERE WERE PLANS TO COMMEMORATE HIM ON A COIN.

LIBERTY

IN GOD WE TRUST

1946

THE ROOSEVELT DIME

IS A NOD TO HIS WORK FIGHTING POLIO WITH THE MARCH OF DIMES.

LOST HOPES

Roosevelt had met with British Prime Minister Winston Churchill on a warship back in August, 1941, seeking to set out the values that could win the public for the bitter war already underway in Europe and soon to involve the United States as well. Their declared purpose and goals were called the Atlantic Charter. It called for all peoples to live in freedom from fear, want and tyranny: these were universals to be denied no one on the planet.

Roosevelt delivered a corollary promise to Americans on January 12, 1944, a State of the Union address that had to be delivered by radio, because of his intensifying illness. The time had come, he insisted, for a second Bill of Rights because the "political rights" guaranteed by the Constitution were inadequate to "assure us equality in the pursuit of happiness." His proposals included a job with a living wage for all; freedom from unfair competition and monopolies; and the right to a home, to medical care, to education and recreation. All these rights, he said in closing, added up to real security, and pointed America toward "new goals of human happiness and well being." The status the United States occupied in the postwar world depended, furthermore, largely on "how these and similar rights have been carried into practice for all our citizens."

Notwithstanding the rapid expansion of the economy, the ideal of equal access to most of these "rights" was never accepted by Republicans, conservative Democrats and many cautiously liberal Democrats. The prospects for enactment and even the memory of FDR's large vision would be swiftly abandoned during the decade following his death.

The fate of the New Deal legacy might be measured somewhat more precisely in the surviving key element of Roosevelt's legislative program, the Full Employment Bill of 1945. Stating that "all Americans able to work and seeking work have the right to useful, remunerative, regular and full time employment," it would, if passed have completed one generation's dream. All those who were willing to work would be rewarded, if necessary through deficit spending or taxation upon the more fortunate. Conservatives predictably blasted the bill, and the wave of anticommunism building up since the middle of the war added to this sentiment. The Employment Act of 1946 spoke only of "maximum employment," a decisive dilution of the original dream.

Three generations later, such a measure has never been enacted. It was an apt symbol for hopes lost, after so much had been gained.

Millions of those alive as adults or children on the day of Roosevelt's death could, decades to come, remember their own personal lives at that moment. Future generations would continue to mull the meanings the New Deal as a manifestation of Franklin Roosevelt's aura—partly because no future president was remotely like FDR. There would be presidents from wealthy families, but none from "Old Wealth," a family with a long history of political leadership. Likewise, there would be reformers or would-be reformers seeking the White House, the most successful perhaps Lyndon B. Johnson, an ardent New Deal supporter in his younger years. But none would enact such sweeping economic and social changes actually challenging business leadership and stressing the primacy of human rights over profits. Nor were conservatives, including those determined to end Social Security altogether or turn its funds into a stock market scheme, able to wipe away all that the New Deal had created.

Perhaps Roosevelt's otherwise keen political sense had failed him most in his acceptance of contemporary liberal and business views of world affairs. Former president Herbert Hoover, always a critic of Roosevelt, believed the postwar determination to control the fate of Europe was a dangerous error. Republican Senator Robert Taft, a deep-hued conservative on all issues, insisted that the determination of Roosevelt's successor to dominate the planet at large through military means was catastrophic, not only in itself but in giving any U.S. president too much power. FDR's expansion of the federal government, especially in worse hands, contained great potential dangers to individual freedom. Lewis Mumford among others had pointed to the alternative solutions of a regional, self-sustaining American economy rather than one bent upon exports and control of both foreign markets and of distant natural resources like oil, lying under the feet of other peoples. Roosevelt did not see these dangers or he did not comprehend their potential.

What would FDR have thought of the grand reform campaign of Barack Obama in 2008, and the tangle of politics after the election? He might have perceived that even the greatest ideals are endangered in the process of realization.

Afterword

141

Harvey Pekar on FDR's New Deal

FDR and the New Deal For Beginners, written by Paul Buhle with comic pages by Sabrina Jones, offers a novel approach to the problems of understanding the New Deal, both as history and as a lesson for today's world.

The Depression of the 1930s, unprecedented in scale and duration, prompted the creation of social programs equally unprecedented. During the generations since, conservatives and sometimes liberals as well have sought to chip away at entitlement programs, loosen control upon financial institutions, and eradicate entirely the egalitarian spirit that infused the best of the New Deal 1930s. But the military-industrial complex expanded in peacetime for perpetuity by President Harry Truman owed its immediate origins to Roosevelt's "Dr. Win the War" final term. Most if not all of the elements ripe for corruption and expansion into a total system can be found here.

There was so much more in the New Deal promise, captured in the pages above. For instance, the Tennessee Valley Authority, a government program that brought electricity to wide rural areas and was the largest single supplier of electric power by 1944. Or the Works Progress Administration's projects to create public arts, from accessible theater to public murals, lithographs, prints and far beyond. Aging former slaves would never have been interviewed about life in the South before the Emancipation Proclamation, if not for New Deal initiatives.

The author and artist of this volume are to be congratulated for highlighting the dynamic driving forces of the New Deal emerging from the bottom tiers of American life. The rent strikes, farm holidays, general strikes in cities, the sit-downs, the rise of industrial unions, anti-fascist popular movements among blue collar ethnic groups—all these forces pushed the President and New Dealers leftward, to places they might not have gone otherwise on their own.

But this book's strongest feature may be the dramatization of the most memorable president of the twentieth century, along with his wife Eleanor Roosevelt, and of the personalities immediately around them, from Harry Hopkins and Henry Wallace to democracy's real enemy from within government, J. Edgar Hoover. The

New Deal years come alive, through the words and the art, as those who lived through the time might remember. Studs Terkel called his classic Depression work *Hard Times*, and they certainly were. But some of the best things about American life took shape then, and remain at risk all these years later. We need to be reminded how the powers of privilege were beaten back, and how they might be beaten back once more.

Bibliography

Paul Buhle and Dave Wagner, *Radical Hollywood: The Untold Story Behind America's Favorite Movies* (New York: New Press, 2002).

Blanche Cook, *Eleanor Roosevelt*, 2 volumes (New York: Viking, 1992, 1999).

John Morton Blum, *V Was for Victory* (New York: Harcourt, Brace, 1977).

John C. Culver and John Hyde, *American Dreamer: The Life and Times of Henry A. Wallace* (New York: Norton, 2000).

Michael Denning, *The Cultural Front: The Laboring of American Culture in the Twentieth Century* (London: Verso Books, 1997).

William D. Hassett, *Off the Record with FDR, 1942-1945* (New Brunswick: Rutgers University Press, 1958).

David M. Kennedy, *Freedom from Fear: The American People in Depression and War, 1929-1945* (New York: Oxford University Press, 1999).

Lash, Joseph, *Eleanor and Franklin* (New York: Norton, 1971).

Ronald Edsforth, *The New Deal* (Boston: Blackwell, 2000).

Robert S. McElvaine, *The Great Depression* (New York: Times Books, 1984).

Kevin J. McMahon, *Reconsidering Roosevelt on Race: How the Presidency Paved the Road to Brown* (Chicago: University of Chicago Press, 2004).

Jean Edward Smith, *FDR* (New York: Random House, 2007).

Ronald Takaki, *Double Victory: A Multicultural History of America in World War II* (Boston: Little, Brown, 2000).

Nick Taylor, *American-Made: The Enduring Legacy of the WPA—When FDR Put America to Work* (New York: Bantam, 2008).

Studs Terkel, *Hard Times: An Oral History of the Great Depression* (New York: Pantheon Books, 1970).

Rexford Tugwell, *The Democratic Roosevelt: a Biography of Franklin D. Roosevelt* (Garden City: Doubleday, 1957).

Geoffrey C. Ward, *Before the Trumpet: Young Franklin Roosevelt, 1882-1905* (New York: Harper & Row, 1985).

William Appleman Williams, *The Contours of American History* (Cleveland: World Publishing Company, 1961).

William Appleman Williams, *Some Presidents: Wilson to Nixon* (New York: New York Review of Books, 1972).

Donald Young, ed., *Adventure in Politics: the Memoirs of Philip La Follette* (New York: Holt, Rinehart and Winston, 1970).

Acknowledgments and Credits

Our thanks go first to Merrilee Warholak, for encouraging and accepting the new-minted conception of an illustrated history book featuring comic art. Next, we wish to thank Phil Hanrahan for his astute copyediting, and finally, David Janik for his insightful and painstaking design.

Apart from the drawings by Bits Hayden appearing on pp. 21, 23, 86, 110 and 116, all taken from *On the Drumhead: A Selection from the Writing of Mike Quin* (San Francisco: Pacific Publishing Foundation, 1948), and the drawings by Sabrina Jones on pp. 13, 23 and 35, the illustrations come from the pages of the magazine *The New Masses*, of the 1930s to middle 1940s.

About the Author and Illustrator

Paul Buhle, recently retired as a Senior Lecturer at Brown University, has written or edited forty-two books including a series of nonfiction comic art volumes in collaboration with Harvey Pekar (*The Beats*); adaptations of works by Howard Zinn (*A People's History of American Empire*) and Studs Terkel (*Studs Terkel's* Working); and authorized biographies on figures such as *Mad Magazine* founder Harvey Kurtzman (*The Art of Harvey Kurtzman*). He has also written on a wide range of subjects in the *Nation, Village Voice, Chronicle of Higher Education* and the *Guardian* (UK). He lives in Madison, and is a Distinguished Scholar of the Organization of American Historical Association and the American Studies Association.

Sabrina Jones wrote and illustrated *Isadora Duncan, A Graphic Biography*. She is a longtime editor and contributor to the political comic book *World War 3 Illustrated*. In the 1990s she co-founded *Girltalk*, an anthology of women's autobiographical comics. She has created nonfiction comics for *Wobblies! A Graphic History of the Industrial Workers of the World;* Studs Terkel's *Working: A Graphic Adaptation; The Real Cost of Prisons* and *Mixed Signals,* a counter-recruitment tool in comic book form. A member of United Scenic Artists local USA 829, she paints scenery for Saturday Night Live.

Afterword:

Harvey Pekar is a comic book writer and author of the autobiographical *American Splendor* series, which was adapted into an Academy Award-nominated film. He lives in Cleveland, Ohio.

THE FOR BEGINNERS® SERIES

AFRICAN HISTORY FOR BEGINNERS:	ISBN 978-1-934389-18-8
ANARCHISM FOR BEGINNERS:	ISBN 978-1-934389-32-4
ARABS & ISRAEL FOR BEGINNERS:	ISBN 978-1-934389-16-4
ART THEORY FOR BEGINNERS:	ISBN 978-934389-47-8
ASTRONOMY FOR BEGINNERS:	ISBN 978-934389-25-6
AYN RAND FOR BEGINNERS:	ISBN 978-1-934389-37-9
BARACK OBAMA FOR BEGINNERS, AN ESSENTIAL GUIDE:	ISBN 978-1-934389-44-7
BLACK HISTORY FOR BEGINNERS:	ISBN 978-1-934389-19-5
THE BLACK HOLOCAUST FOR BEGINNERS:	ISBN 978-1-934389-03-4
BLACK WOMEN FOR BEGINNERS:	ISBN 978-1-934389-20-1
CHOMSKY FOR BEGINNERS:	ISBN 978-1-934389-17-1
DADA & SURREALISM FOR BEGINNERS:	ISBN 978-1-934389-00-3
DECONSTRUCTION FOR BEGINNERS:	ISBN 978-1-934389-26-3
DEMOCRACY FOR BEGINNERS:	ISBN 978-1-934389-36-2
DERRIDA FOR BEGINNERS:	ISBN 978-1-934389-11-9
EASTERN PHILOSOPHY FOR BEGINNERS:	ISBN 978-1-934389-07-2
EXISTENTIALISM FOR BEGINNERS:	ISBN 978-1-934389-21-8
FOUCAULT FOR BEGINNERS:	ISBN 978-1-934389-12-6
GLOBAL WARMING FOR BEGINNERS:	ISBN 978-1-934389-27-0
HEIDEGGER FOR BEGINNERS:	ISBN 978-1-934389-13-3
ISLAM FOR BEGINNERS:	ISBN 978-1-934389-01-0
KIERKEGAARD FOR BEGINNERS:	ISBN 978-1-934389-14-0
LACAN FOR BEGINNERS:	ISBN 978-1-934389-39-3
LINGUISTICS FOR BEGINNERS:	ISBN 978-1-934389-28-7
MALCOLM X FOR BEGINNERS:	ISBN 978-1-934389-04-1
NIETZSCHE FOR BEGINNERS:	ISBN 978-1-934389-05-8
THE OLYMPICS FOR BEGINNERS:	ISBN 978-1-934389-33-1
PHILOSOPHY FOR BEGINNERS:	ISBN 978-1-934389-02-7
PLATO FOR BEGINNERS:	ISBN 978-1-934389-08-9
POETRY FOR BEGINNERS:	ISBN 978-1-934389-46-1
POSTMODERNISM FOR BEGINNERS:	ISBN 978-1-934389-09-6
RELATIVITY & QUANTUM PHYSICS FOR BEGINNERS	ISBN 978-1-934389-42-3
SARTRE FOR BEGINNERS:	ISBN 978-1-934389-15-7
SHAKESPEARE FOR BEGINNERS:	ISBN 978-1-934389-29-4
STRUCTURALISM & POSTSTRUCTURALISM FOR BEGINNERS:	ISBN 978-1-934389-10-2
ZEN FOR BEGINNERS:	ISBN 978-1-934389-06-5
ZINN FOR BEGINNERS:	ISBN 978-1-934389-40-9

www.forbeginnersbooks.com